Tim

Time

The Modern and Postmodern Experience

Helga Nowotny

Translated by Neville Plaice

Polity Press

This translation copyright © Polity Press 1994.
First published in German as *Eigenzeit Entstehung und Strukturierung eines Zeitgefühls* copyright © Suhrkamp Verlag, Frankfurt am Main, 1989.
Foreword copyright © J. T. Fraser 1994.

First published in 1994 by Polity Press
in association with Blackwell Publishers Ltd.
First published in paperback 1996.

Editorial office:
Polity Press
65 Bridge Street
Cambridge CB2 1UR, UK

Marketing and production:
Blackwell Publishers Ltd
108 Cowley Road
Oxford OX4 1JF, UK

Blackwell Publishers Inc.
238 Main Street
Cambridge, MA 02142, USA

ISBN 0–7456–0892–2
ISBN 0–7456–1837–5 (pbk)

A CIP catalogue record for this book is available from the British Library and the Library of Congress.

Typeset in 11 on 12½ pt Plantin
by Best-set Typesetter Ltd., Hong Kong
Printed in Great Britain by T.J. Press (Padstow) Ltd, Padstow, Cornwall.

This book is printed on acid-free paper.

Contents

An Embarrassment of Proper Times:
A Foreword

J. T. Fraser

Great changes in scientific understanding tend to rever-
berate across the cultural fabric of their epochs. The
Copernican revolution inspired rich literary and artistic
expressions, as did Newton's formulation of the law of
gravitation. In this century Albert Einstein placed the laws
of motion, force and electricity into a mathematically uni-
fied framework called space-time. One of the new concepts introduced in his Relativity Theory, that of 'the
fourth dimension', entered the vocabulary of daily discourse and of the media. Through the alchemy of the
collective and individual creation of ideas, the term
worked its way into public awareness as a metaphor for the
scientific understanding of the nature of time.

In *Time: The Modern and Postmodern Experience*, Helga
Nowotny, a distinguished Austrian sociologist of science
and President of the International Society for the Study of
Time (1992–5), analyses the social changes of our age in
terms of the idea and experience of time. She makes
imaginative and fruitful use of 'proper time', a concept
which originated in Relativity Theory, as did 'the fourth
dimension'.

The German word for proper time is *Eigenzeit*. This is
also the title of Professor Nowotny's book, of which the

present volume is a translation. *Eigen* means 'belonging to the self'. Verbatim, *Eigenzeit* means 'self-time'; *Eigenliebe*, 'self-love'. To those who read German, the meaning of *eigen* in its many combinations is obvious. Because of this obviousness the word *Eigenzeit* is well suited to imply, in German, a formal linkage between designating temporalities appropriate for the Theory of Relativity (where its precise meaning needs extended explanation) and those appropriate for social science (where its meaning is almost, though not totally, self-evident).

Early in the history of Relativity Theory *Eigenzeit* was translated into English as *Eigen*-time, together with such related technical terms as *Eigen*-function and *Eigen*-value. Later, the word *Eigen* was replaced by 'proper' to yield the names proper time, proper function and proper value. 'Proper' is a cognate in English of *Eigen*, as in 'property' (*Eigentum*) or in the proper days of the saints in the Roman calendar. But while the translation is accurate, the self-evidence of the word and, with it, the hint of some formal kinship between certain physical and social aspects of time are absent. Had Professor Nowotny's book *Eigenzeit* appeared under the title *Proper Time*, it would have suggested a work on etiquette for British high tea rather than a treatise on the sociology of time.

What does proper time mean in physics and in this book?

In Relativity Theory it is the time span between two events in the life of a clock as measured by that clock. So far this is only a definition, and not even a very interesting one. It becomes more interesting when one considers two clocks in relative motion, and outright intriguing when the clocks are the biological cycles of living organisms. It is under such conditions that the distinction between time and proper time may be illustrated. Here is an example.

Consider an Indian elephant with its gestation period of 645 days and a house mouse with her 19 days. Let each female mate with her respective male on 1 January. Then, let the mouse go on an extended round trip at very large velocities, with her itinerary designed by a competent relativist. Let her return on 7 October of the next year, just in time to celebrate the simultaneous delivery of the two offsprings. The temporal separation between the twin events (the begetting and delivering of the infants) was 15,480 hours in the elephant's proper time, 456 hours in the proper time of the mouse.

With current transportation technology such a trip would be impossible, but the principles are valid. Each of the two time measurements must be regarded as real and correct. And each is an invariant quantity. Here invariance means that anyone who knows Einstein's instructions on how to calculate time at a distance – no matter where the measurer is or how she or he moves – will obtain the figures of 15,480 and 456 hours, respectively, for the proper times of the two animals. These numbers, correlated through certain equations, cohere in seamless unity upon a higher level of generalization than is possible to attain through Newtonian theory. All this holds even though there is nothing in Relativity Theory that could tell us what is to be meant by the now, the future, the past or the flow of time. The physicist has to know what time is before he or she can begin experimenting with travelling elephants and mice.

During the trip, the flow of time will retain its hallmarks for each animal. Their days will pass through instants of changing presents, with respect to which future and past acquire meaning. And a three-minute egg will need three minutes of boiling.

The need for thinking in terms of proper times arises only when one wishes to make comparisons between time measurements performed in two or more systems in relative motion. The whole conceptual scheme becomes necessary only if the elephant wanted to know how long, in her proper time, did the mouse take to make her three-minute egg? Time, so to say, is the set; proper times are the members of the set.

Let us now map these ideas about time, proper time and their relationships into the study of social processes.

Unlike in physics, proper times in Professor Nowotny's book differ qualitatively, not by the quantities of time units. Proper time stands for a constellation of beliefs regarding future, past and present, for opinions about change and permanence, about the inevitability of death, about philosophical, religious and aesthetic judgements, and even about identities and allegiances. It stands for the totality of a person's or group's ideas and experiences of time.

Professor Nowotny maintains that it is social organization from which people draw their fundamental thought categories, such as space and time. If so, then it is not surprising that the social whirlwind of our age becomes manifest in the appearance of a large variety of proper times. Individuals and societies no less than commercial, industrial, political and ideological interest groups have their own proper times. That is, they have differing judgements about the role and importance of their own and of other people's and groups' times. Whether as abstract ideas or guidelines for action, all these proper times are in ceaseless conflict or, more precisely, the persons and groups maintaining those proper times are. Such differences have surely existed all through history but they have become noticeable, then interesting, and finally significant because of the time-compactness of the globe with its cultural and ethnic diversity.

This is a book of keen observations about a restless age, and one full of inspiring epigrams. In spite or perhaps because of that restlessness, writes the author, the search for an understanding of the patterns of social change remains an attractive task. It is a fascinating one, not simply because it helps us to take successful action in social life, a process still inscrutable, but, more basically, because there is a human need to be able to discover the beauty of regularities beyond the will and intention of human beings.

In the rich tapestry of change surveyed in the book, modernism emerges as a turn-of-the-nineteenth-century syndrome, as well as a moving force for the advancement of the artificial in the service of society. Postmodernism is a post-Second World War phenomenon. It may best be described as a reflection of changes which are so rapid as to make their integration into the recent past and onrushing future impossible. The environment created by individuals and societies thus outruns the adaptive capacities of their creators and leads to a loss of temporal horizons or, as Professor Nowotny calls it, the extended present.

It is along this path of understanding that the social interpretation of proper time proves itself to be helpful in elucidating the global problems of our age.

Introduction

> Time talks. It speaks more plainly than words. The message it
> conveys comes through loud and clear. Because it is manipulated
> less consciously, it is subject to less distortion than the spoken
> language. It can shout the truth where words lie.
>
> E. T. Hall, *The Silent Language*

Everyone is a practician and theoretician of time. Time
'dwells' in us – through the biological rhythms to which we
are subject, and because we are social beings who are born
into a society with changing temporal structures and learn
to live in its social time. But the knowledge people have
about the time which flows, periodically returns, ends and
begins in them – time which can produce moments of
unforgettable intensity, but also of pain and emptiness –
remains strangely embroiled in their own consciousness
and in their personal temporal world. Although we share
time with others (or complain that others do not have
enough time for us or we for them), the discursive exchange about time is underdeveloped. Most metaphors
concerning time reflect the experiences of earlier generations, not our own experiences. It is as if language
absorbs only with delay what social experience seeks to
confide to it. And it is as if time, filtered through institutions and regulated in temporal systems, conveyed
through machines and means of transport, confronts us as
'a very strange thing' (as Hofmannsthal makes the
Marschallin say in *Der Rosenkavalier*) which is able to exert
a curious compulsion over people. In his essay on time,
Norbert Elias has referred to the masks which many tribal

societies exhibit in their rituals. For the participants in the ceremony, the masks are endowed with social reality; they are gods or demons, even though everyone knows that behind them there are people moving them. In a similar way, the mask of the clock and the appointments diary also encourages us to think they embody time which passes without our agency and cannot be arrested. We believe we have to be governed by them, whereas they merely reproduce series of movements which are shaped as symbols in such a way that we are able to orient the coordination of our own activities by them. For it is we human beings who make time. The more complex the society, the more stratified the courses of time also become which overlap, form temporal connections with and alongside one another. Perhaps the raising of the mask, the diagnostic glance at its operation, and the effect which results from it, is the most effective challenge for a (social) scientific study of time. Time has become a fundamental issue for all sciences, since it raises problems central to the understanding of the phenomena under investigation. Coping with the problem of 'time' often opens up those boundaries of a theory which stimulate further development, as Prigogine and Stengers have recently demonstrated in relation to physics.[1] But the complaint often heard that time is a neglected topic in the social sciences is not true. The libraries are full of detailed and also of general investigations. Admittedly, the longer-term social processes have been somewhat lost sight of, and in view of the tendency to label society boldly, the contribution of individuals to society is neglected. But time hardly takes account of the drawing up of disciplinary and other boundaries, just as it is hardly possible to capture and to fix it in everyday life.

My interest focuses on the question: how does time change? It all began many years ago with my desire to know why some people have 'more', others 'less', and many 'no' time at all, and how these differences were

connected with the culture from which they came, with
their class status and the relations they established with
past, present and future.[2] Then in the course of time many
new questions and observations were added: women's
time is differently structured and is used differently from
men's time; the phenomenon of 'everyday life', in which
the boundaries between private and public time are increasingly beginning to become blurred, also began to
interest me. I gradually became convinced of the inexor-
able disappearance of the category of the future and its
replacement by something I call the extended present.
And always and everywhere I encountered those technologies which are changing the human perception of time
most immediately and most visibly – the modern technologies of communication. Their influence is perceptible,
tangible, and demonstrable at work and at home, in means
of transport and in communication networks, in the
finance markets of the world and in the countries of the
Third World.

Thus, over a period of years, this essay gradually took
shape. It is sustained by the wish to come up with a fairly
sound social scientific diagnosis of the current changes in
the concept of time, but also in the experience of time and
the conflicts about time, a diagnosis which is intended to
open up knowledge to current everyday life. The subjective awareness of individuals about what is happening in
them and with them timewise can be communicated to
others only in fragmentary form. What the social sciences
are able to contribute is the establishment of those fine
links which reveal 'society' in the experience of every
individual. Like a test liquid which flows through the body
to detect particular substances and their courses, 'society'
and social time run through a life, however individually
distinctive and equipped it is. For time, this symbolic
product of human coordination and ascription of significance, collectively shaped and moulded at a deep level,
retains its relation to others even at moments of distinctive

individual feeling. Even the time of the lonely is merely a lack of jointly spent, of shared time. And the lack of time, in turn, is proportionate to the wealth of socially moulded expectations and the standards of one's own behaviour.

The diagnosis made it necessary to select perspectives, to restrict observations and to use them in dependence on particular tools of thought. Many associations with the topic which readers may have will not be dealt with here. Above all the realm of individual psychology has been omitted, not because it is less worthy of attention, but because it seemed to me more urgent to demonstrate the connections with social changes. Questions of the formation of identity, of the relationship between the generations and of the process of ageing, for which the topic of time is of central importance, are likewise dealt with only marginally.[3] Instead, I talk about the ageing of technologies. The fascinating area of the cultural variety of conceptions of time has also had to be left out. The confrontation with non-Western time-cultures and their wealth of distinctions is gaining urgency in view of the economic and technological processes with which a time-culture born in the West is preparing to embrace the whole earth. But my own present, however much I tried to extend it, was not sufficient to transcend the geographical space of time familiar to me.

The qualitative changes in the perception of time, in the sense of time and in the social and individual structuring of time, which are dealt with in the following chapters, are manifestly expressed in the technologies striving for a world-wide condition of simultaneity. Are not the great financial markets of London, Tokyo, New York and Singapore connected with one another right round the clock? Is it not possible at any time, from any place on the earth, to send news to someone else, to exchange information, to carry out transactions? Yet behind the high-rise offices fashioned in glass with their air-conditioning there dwells in most international cities an indescribable misery.

The village without a sanitary and medical infrastructure is just as far or as little removed from the most up-to-date computer system as is the latter from the terminals connected with it. Making an approximative simultaneity possible with the aid of modern electronics has by no means led to a social simultaneity. On the contrary, new inequalities are arising from non-simultaneities. Paradoxically, the gap which separates developing countries from the industrial nations with their technological and economic advantage is growing to the same extent that temporal and spatial distances are shrinking.

The discovery of simultaneity as a phenomenon of the perception of time and its real, economic and technological implementation are at the centre of the first chapter. They lend the connection between power and time a qualitatively new dimension. Whoever governs simultaneity controls the temporal dependences derivable from it. Yet despite the attainment of ever higher speeds in the networking of information technology, despite the continuing expansion of the technological infrastructure which installs simultaneity, it remains an illusion. In a certain sense it replaces the horizon of the future which has sustained the belief in progress over the last two hundred years, as the discrepancy between experience and the expectation of constant improvements which keeps on renewing itself and strives towards an open future. The greater the approximation to simultaneity, the more the little temporal differences count. As in sport, where tenths and hundredths of a second have long decided victory or defeat, in the international competition for markets and advantages in technological innovation it is the little temporal discrepancies which bring profit and further advantages. Such a simultaneity institutionalized world-wide, with its discrepancies calculated to produce dependences by means of non-simultaneity, also has consequences for the quality of time itself. While in the phase of industrialization it was above all the equation of time and money which resulted from the industrial capitalist logic of production and made time a scarce commodity, time is now being speeded up itself: it is becoming accelerated innovation.

The disappearance of the future and the extension of the present taking its place are the subject of the second chapter. The drawing up of the boundary between the temporal periods which mark past, present and future is not a universally valid one. Society and its members judge it differently and in each case project into it their hopes and their problems and contradictions unsolved with regard to time. With the end of an age in which, by means of the time-structure of industrial production, both linearity and the belief in progress were sustained, the category of the future is losing much of its attractiveness. A present geared to accelerated innovation is beginning to devour the future. Problems which could formerly be deferred into the future reach into the present for their part, press for solutions which admittedly may not be on the agenda until tomorrow but demand to be dealt with today. The permeability of the time-boundary between present and future is increased by technologies which facilitate temporal uncoupling and decentralization, and which produce different models of time referring to the present that have largely become detached from linearity. But the process of continual 'creative destruction', as Schumpeter called the business of innovation, leads to another problem of civilization: that of obsolescence, the ageing of technologies, the production of waste. The past cannot absorb the waste fast enough. Through the creation of more and more new things, there is an inevitable increase of that which has to be disposed of. Both processes require a changed balance – in an extended present.

But what is it that so relentlessly drives on the civilization of scientific technology in terms of time, that generates the insatiable need for what is new, a need which presses for even more acceleration? This is the question posed in the third chapter. If it is true that the linear continuum, which entered the so-called modern era with the belief in progress from the eighteenth century on, has broken down, if time 'has died', as some writers and philosophers see it, that time which was based on the continuum at least, what takes its place? Is it the moment which, detached from perpetual continuity, is enhanced into the source of hope that time can be stopped, which makes interim periods possible that are not subject to the flow of the linear continuum? Or is the continuum with its built-in acceleration replaced by a new time-cycle, this time marked by technological recurrence, in the form of the long waves of the Kondratiev business cycle or its variants?

From a scientific and technological point of view, the acceleration of the process of innovation can be reconstructed. It is connected with the temporal conditions which can be artificially produced in the science laboratory, and with the temporal and spatial possibilities of scientific work by means of which natural phenomena can be kept temporally available in the laboratory. Other time-structures are thereby induced which continue to have an innovative effect. Scientific and technological innovations strive for the unexpected and attempt to plan it none the less. They would like to anticipate the consequent effects, but with the emergence of the newly created objects from the laboratory and through their entry into social reality, they also move into another temporal domain.

The theme of proper time runs through several chapters. The history of the time-givers, above all the clock, reflects the relationship of human beings in their temporal limitation between their social environment and their 'own', individualized time which develops only gradually. Clocks as time-givers also embody the values of a society. The first clocks had little in common with the functional time-givers which show values today that have long since been made international. With the emergence of bourgeois society, in which subjectivity gradually became a new point of reference, there also arose the partial release from a common, social time. For the first time it became possible for the female reader of a novel to absent herself in time and to transpose herself to an imaginary world also temporally detached from social reality. In the world of the bourgeoisie, the public time of work was set against the private time within the family. Both were temporally regulated, with precisely specifiable rites of transition. In this polarization there arose a specific I-time-perspective which knew how to distinguish between one's own time (proper time) and that of others. With the intensification of working life and increasing pressure of time, but above all with the emergence of women from the private time of the family and their participation in the public time of working life, there grew the desire for a new category of disposal: disposal of one's own time, rights to which are declared, as if it were a question of acquiring possession of it.

Such a configuration brings with it conflicts and problems of distribution. The fourth chapter deals with them. Time has become the subject of politics. Urgent questions about the distribution of work and of time within a society in which the former became the prerequisite for the latter break with unquestioned conventions and shake the established distinctions between work and free time. The complex and increasing significance which time has gained for people today in their different situations in life and phases of life finds its expression in equally different time-preferences. There thus arises a conflict-laden co-existence, having many associations, of time-cultures and desires for better coordination and synchronization, for fairer patterns of distribution in an everyday life in which private time and public time are vaguely mixed.

What new patterns of distribution could look like, what social uchronias arise from the unsolved problems and what solutions there may be, are summarized in the final chapter. It is about action in time, about people playing with time. People create time through their cooperation and their coexistence, their diachronic interconnections beyond time and through their synchronic relations *in* time. The time of action always contains elements of decision; it is confronted with the uncertainty of the outcome. Trust presupposes expectations of a longer-lasting relationship, it is based on expected durability. Short-term interactions negate time, and where time is neglected, responsibility also dwindles. The separate development of every human being is codetermined by that point at which he or she joins the stream of social development; self-awareness, tools of thought, concepts and perceptions are marked by a stamp of historicity specific to one's generation. But this is equally true of the coming generations to whom a world is bequeathed which they have not yet been able to shape. Is more thinking necessary in intergenerational categories, in view of the momentum which is produced by human intervention in the natural environment? What scope for action in time is there for timely action?

Time is always also a strategic concept. There is timing in everything, even if the verb 'to time' is not to be found in the German language. In the conflicts between the super-powers, in the international rivalry of firms and nations, in the chronogram of every organization which has to decide whether it should expand or not, the choice of the 'right' moment is important. Learning to handle one's own reserves of time better in the face of a limited term of life, resisting the pressure of time, presupposes an appreciative openness towards the strategically playful aspect in time. Some things may be learnable in seminars on time management, but there are innumerable playful approaches and strategies. It seems important to me to learn to understand the temporal frameworks and rhythms of the social background, the rules to which timing is subject in each society. Only against the background of speed can slowness be determined and learnt. Only against the background of temporal limitation can the latter be surpassed.

The previous history of the Western linear system of time is closely connected with industrialization and the brutal adaptation of human labour and life to the machine. The exploitation of the resources of time which had been made scarce led first to painful wear and tear – in the hope of a better future. Today the future has caught up with the present, but time, individually and collectively, has remained limited. New resources of time are in demand. They are opening up through the extension of time in the present and through the availability at all times which technologies make possible. But the latter in their turn demand a temporal availability of human beings. So where is the time to be found?

There thus arises the longing for the moment. In strategic terms, it has to be the 'right' moment. In playful creative terms, it is the moment which – for a short time – makes everything possible, and from which history flows.

Seeking the moment and finding it ultimately means acknowledging one's own temporality.

For the genesis of this essay, many temporal prerequisites were necessary. Two of them can also be designated in spatial and institutional terms. I would like to thank Clemens Heller, who invited me to the Maison des Sciences de l'Homme in Paris in February 1987, and the Rockefeller Foundation, as whose guest at the conference centre in Bellagio I was able to complete this text.

Helga Nowotny
Bellagio, August 1988

1

The Illusion of Simultaneity

Except for light switches nothing worked by pushing a button.
The phonograph had to be wound, a lot of the cars had to be
cranked, coffee was ground by cranking, too, and the hand still
had uses beyond separating pieces of paper money and pointing.
Arthur Miller, *Timebends*

At the turn of the twelfth to the thirteenth century, something began to stir in Europe. 'Eight hundred years ago',
writes Adolf Holl, 'people in some European cities began
to feel a strange and previously unheard-of desire. They
wanted to know the time.'[1] God's time, as the French historian LeGoff put it, gave way to the time of the traders.
What was dawning was a premonition of a future which
would prove to be open to the human creative capacity. A
future which involved risks, for only someone prepared to
risk his or her assets again and again for the sake of an
opportunity was able to head for this horizon. With the
eighteenth century, the horizon of the future became dynamic. The idea of progress entered the history of the
human race and temporalized it. Today the tension between present experience that does not value what is past
and an expectation oriented towards what is, in tendency,
endless improvement has largely collapsed. The belief in
progress in the last two hundred years has been severely
shaken. But the need for time, which the natural sciences
first declared with the Enlightenment when they included
in their programme the achievement of what is new, and
hence, according to Hans Blumenberg, opened up the 'divide
between lifetime and world time', has continued to grow.

What has also increased, however, is precision in the measurement of time, which can be conducted with the aid of caesium atomic clocks. Time has become a unit of measurement per se, to which other fundamental measurements, above all the measurement of length, are reduced. For some time now, it has been specified as the unit of time which light covers within a certain time. The human brain perceives space via time differences established by the nervous system. The accuracy of gauges in physics makes it possible to detect variations and small irregularities where one previously saw constants. Thus we know today that the period of the earth's rotation, which before 1967 served as a basis for the measurement of time, varies slightly between summer and winter, and from year to year. These variations are partly regular, partly unpredictable. World time is established by an international clock authority, the Bureau International de l'Heure in Paris, on the basis of the readings which come from the largest measuring laboratories in the world. At intervals of about one and a half years, so-called leap seconds are inserted into the coordinated universal time, of the UTC, to prevent deviations of more than 0.7 seconds from navigational time from arising.[2] The range of the measurement of time within physics contains periods which extend from 10–15 thousand million years (the time light requires to reach the earth from the remotest still observable galaxy, which indicates the age of the known universe as well) to 10^{-15} seconds (e.g. for phenomena in the atomic sphere). But phenomena are also investigated which require even less time, for instance the duration of elemental processes which can be imagined down to 10^{-44} seconds (Planck's scale).

Everyday life in society has a different look to that in physics. In social life, time-scales are used which are suitable to human behaviour and human perception. They range from the mythical times of the 'once upon a time' to the immediately perceptible present, and can accordingly be indicated in tens of thousands of years or in split seconds. Infinitely long or infinitesimally short periods are experienced as larger or smaller in relation to the human perceptive faculty. But in social existence as well, the precision of the measurement of time has been refined and the temporal range extended. It is not just that past and future have been extended in the footsteps of the periods of time opened up by the measurements of physics – a spatial extension of a standardized time, gradually encompassing the earth, has also taken place. A lot of things have contributed to this: the processes of increasing economic and political integration and the technological possibilities which provide the transport of goods, people and information more quickly and on a broader basis, but also a gradual alignment of ways of life which began with the industrial mode of production. The insistence on a standardization of time in social life manifests itself in the approach towards a world-wide simultaneity, the perception of events and of processes which occur at the same time in different corners of the earth. Today people again feel a peculiar and hitherto unheard-of desire: *they want to have more time for themselves.*

What leads people to declare their pressing need for time so categorically, especially in this pronounced first person form? After all, they have got their time-saving machines which make their lives easier and relieve them of tedious or heavy manual work. Means of transport are always available to take them at great speed to almost all corners of the earth. Today many more things work by pushing a button than just the light switches. Modern communication technologies attain speeds which can no longer be directly perceived by human sense organs. But through integration into world-wide simultaneity there grows the need to distinguish one's 'own' time from that which connects people with others; there grows the desire to be able to control the interlocking to some extent oneself, to gain 'temporal sovereignty' over one's local time, which is now visibly and noticeably integrated into world time. It is not so much the very long and the very short time, the time of history, of the 'longue durée' and the specious present, of the perception of the flow of time in split seconds, which seek contact and resolution in a juxtaposition charged with tension, but one's own, subjective local time that sees itself confronted with a public world time which – spatially extended over the entire earth – professes to be simultaneous.

The discovery of the simultaneity installed almost everywhere today, which can transport, exchange and generate world news and stock market prices, financial transactions and television pictures via satellite transmission, first made itself felt, in spectacular fashion, at the turn of the century. As the American cultural historian Stephen Kern has shown in detail, the period between 1880 and 1918 laid the foundations for the drastic changes people experienced in the sense of space and time. It was as if the technological, artistic and scientific achievements of this epoch converged to break down the well-rehearsed spatial and temporal structures of social perception and transform them into a broad experimental field, in which new ways of seeing, different spatial forms and, not least, new, more democratic, social and political relations were to be tested and rehearsed. Spatial distances which had been insurmountable up till then were erased by the invention and regular technological improvements of the telegraph, the radio and the telephone. Through the electrification of the cities, the difference between day and night could be artificially negated for the first time. The cinematograph succeeded not just in making pictures move but in slowing down or speeding up the captured movements at will, indeed even in winding them backwards and thus creating totally new ways of seeing. It is not surprising that it was above all the artists and writers who got swept up in these changes and who attempted to give voice and expression, sound and form to the new sense of space and time. The classical narrative mode of the novel or the conventional stanzas of lyric poetry were rejected, and replaced by revolutionary innovations. The changed sense of time seized hold of music and led to the creation of atonalities never heard before, which were based on the twelve-tone scale. In the plastic and graphic arts and in painting, forms were sought which made it possible to portray several perspectives at the same time; form and colour were to be capable of reproducing the changes from moment to moment. Without any historical exaggeration, it can be said that the remarkable artistic creativity of that period, whose 'intoxication with space and time' was to last far into the inter-war period, drew more or less consciously on the ruins of a declining social system, in which it was no longer true, as formerly, that everything had 'its time and place'. It was rather a question of defining time and place anew, for the greatest possible – and for the first time also democratic – variety of perspectives and points of view, of positions and subjective experiences.[3]

In a different way, space and time – and the perception of them – also moved into the centre of scientific study. In physics, Newton's idea of an absolute space and an absolute time was written off virtually in passing.[4] In thermodynamics, with the thermal death of the universe the temporal vector was stringently formulated for the first time. In 1905, Einstein calculated within the framework of the Special Theory of Relativity how time appears slowed down in a system moving away at constant speed. With the General Theory of Relativity in 1916, he extended the theory to accelerated bodies. Since all matter in the universe produces a gravitational field, and since gravity is equally acceleration, every body has its own time. In a later popularization of his theory, Einstein compares the old mechanics, which only recognized a single clock, with his theory, according to which 'we can imagine as many clocks as we want.'[5] With quantum mechanics, that subjectivist element was introduced into physics which led to the abandonment of a realist description. But does not this subjectivist element, the role which was ascribed to the observer, stem from the fact that the vector of time did not really find its way into the theoretical structure of quantum mechanics, but was merely appended to it, with the aid of the concept of the observer?[6]

Within psychology and the areas of philosophy overlapping with it, questions about the relationship between the subjective perception of time and objective measurability, and the tension between 'internal', experienced time and 'external', given time, were likewise a central preoccupation. Since the 1880s, psychologists had been in search of the duration of the present. The intention was to measure the interval in which time could be perceived by the individual as a continuous whole. But what was this present? Was not that which appears concurrently a succession in the seeing of the object? Was not time more comparable to a flow than to a sum of discrete units? In William James's famous formulation of 1890, the present is 'a stream of thought, of consciousness' and not a 'bucket of water'. The 'specious present' of which James speaks was not comparable with a knife-edge, but was more like a 'saddle-back, with a certain breadth of its own on which we sit perched, and from which we look in two directions into time'.[7] It was more than just a fleeting moment, since it proved dense enough to make it possible to perceive more than just one event, to hear more than just one melody. Past events or perceptions could end, but they remained, as in Husserl, present as 'retentions'. For James Joyce, the condensed present was the only real place in which it was possible to have experiences. Because he gives interior monologues to the hero of his novel Leopold Bloom and his contemporary companions in 'time', who inhabit with him the universe of the streets and pubs of Dublin, and compresses all experiences into those famous sixteen hours on 16 June 1904, the experience of simultaneity is both relativized and objectivized. The question as to whether public time, measurable, objective time, was part of inner awareness or not had found its artistic answer. Even the body can measure time, wrote an enthusiastic critic about Proust's masterpiece. And the two French anthropologists Hubert and Mauss, disciples of Durkheim, gave the following answer:

> The interplay of concepts which psychological reality forms from successive images consists in the matching of two sets of ideas. One is constant and periodical – it is that of the calendar . . . the other continually constructs itself through the act of producing new ideas. The mind is constantly endeavouring to bring together certain elements of these two sets in a single tension.[8]

What preoccupied people at that time, and what scientists and artists had taken up, was the question as to how real their own experience of time was. The more they realized that their own temporal and spatial categories, from a subjective point of view at least, were legitimate, and that there was obviously a public time of the calendar and a private time of their feelings and their body, the more urgent it became to clarify the relationship of these two kinds of time to one another. What sparked the discovery of simultaneity, which presupposed a world organized into time-zones, and which became subjectively comprehensible through communication technologies, was the confrontation between a now standardized public time and the variety of private, subjective times. The discovery became dramatically comprehensible through events like the sinking of the *Titanic*, whose SOS calls were heard by numerous ships within a radius of a hundred nautical miles. The next morning people in capital cities on both sides of the Atlantic could read about the dramatic events at the breakfast table in their newspapers.

The emergence of simultaneity – in contrast to its discovery – had been prepared in longer-term processes. It is first connected with the spatial extension of state control, then with the economic one of the market, and finally with that of technologies. European expansion, indeed expansion in general, first took place over territory. The colonial powers occupied foreign countries, took territorial possession of them. The nation-states within Europe arose in spatially delimited territories, within which they exercised a monopoly on the use of force and the raising of taxes.

Along with spatial control, the temporal kind is also established, but it still completely follows the imperatives of the organizational needs of the central powers: the temporal control of the bureaucracies, which is based on the punctuality that was necessary for maintaining discipline in the army, at school, and later in the factories. The process of diffusion of temporal control breaks away from the static system of time of the big bureaucracies only with the economic boom of capitalism and its expansion. Temporal control is symbolized by the idea of progress, of economic boom. The gap between the capital city and the village which still has no asphalt road or is not yet connected to the national grid is a temporal-economic one. Economic dynamics causes new centres to arise which are ahead of their times, and peripheries which are backward, wherever they may be geographically located. The primary distributive mechanism of this temporal control becomes the market. Calculated to surmount spatial limits, it seems to negate time in the act of buying and yet profits from the small temporal difference, from the advantages over competitors which a few hours, days or months bring in buying or selling. They are what decide on profit and loss. Extending and using these temporal advantages, applying them to many transactions, also became possible spatially over the entire world with the aid of communication technologies. It was not by chance that the first telephones were installed in order to be able to transmit the stock market prices more quickly; the

ceremonial opening of the first lines was left to the head of
state simply as an act of political courtesy. How ex-
tensively the market and technology pervade one another
was strikingly expressed by those photographic images
sent round the world by the media on the occasion of the
stock market crash in autumn 1987. They showed almost
identically dressed stockbrokers, holding at least three
telephones to their ears, who were trying to save what
could be saved in New York and Tokyo. Through the
networking of computers, in which contingent conditions
of purchase and sale were programmed, the standardization of time had reached a new, provisional peak.

Officially, it began unspectacularly and almost, dis-
regarding the consequences, trivially. In 1884 one of
the then numerous international conferences was held
which were striving for a standardization of norms,
weights and measures.[9] Out of practical, commercial and
political necessity, states were pressing for international
agreements which were intended to introduce more clar-
ity, convertibility and rationality into the confusing variety
of local, regional and national standards. No bold utopias
inspired the advocates of standardization, but the sober
calculations of engineers, industrialists, civil servants and
army officers. At the international meridian conference,
the object was to divide the world into twenty-four time-
zones each with an hour's difference and to draw an obligatory international date line. A decision had to be taken
about where 'east' and where 'west' was, since it followed
from this which places in the world would be chronologi-
cally 'ahead of' or 'behind' other places. Such a decision
was arbitrary, of course, but temporal coordination at an
international level could only result if there was a temporal
dividing line which met with international assent. Since
then, the 180th meridian at the same distance east and
west of Greenwich has been regarded as the international
date line. Crossing it eastwards, travellers gain a day, while
in the opposite direction they lose a day. If it is Tuesday

evening in Tokyo, it is Tuesday morning in New York and not Wednesday morning, for instance. Since then, New York has been all of fourteen hours 'behind' Tokyo and not ten hours 'ahead'. The standardization of world time had direct technological and also military benefits. Unlike in the Middle Ages, when it was still customary to be woken for battle by cocks which had been brought along, the machinery of war now also required a coordination which was as accurate as possible. Equally, world time was the condition for the coordination of the many local systems of time with one another, for establishing timetables without which the spatial extension and concentration of the transport network would have been inconceivable.

Historians of technology have described in detail how the first modern technologies overcoming space and time, the telegraph and telephone, radio, but also the cinema, just like the railways before them, did not merely help to reduce geographical distances but conveyed the feeling that social barriers could also be overcome. At the turn of the century, the hierarchical structures of the nobility, but also those of the bourgeois world, had begun to totter. The potential for change, the susceptibility of existing power structures to a 'levelling' technology, was strikingly illustrated by the possibility of disrespectfully crossing bounds of protocol which lay within the capacity of the technological media. It was not by chance that telephones were not admitted to the Imperial Palace in Vienna, typewriters were regarded with mistrust, and electric light was reserved for the streets and the citizens, for they equally threatened a social hierarchy in its fine distinctions, which were also spatially and temporally coordinated.[10] It was obvious that waiting periods could be reduced by the telephone, and that many a ministerial art of processing files would soon become superfluous. For the visionaries of the approaching democracy, it was a question of reducing not just political power distinctions, but cultural ones as well. The cinema, celebrated as the democratic medium per se, made it possible from now on to bring the enjoyment of art and culture, indeed simple entertainment, out of the exclusive court theatres and out of the bourgeois cultural sphere, and to make them available to everybody for little money. It was a period which did not yet suspect what dimensions the saturation with mass media would assume, and that television would literally come to every tin hut. Finally, means of transport, from the railways via the bicycle to the motor-car, opened up free spaces for a society which has since made individual mobility one of its central values. Yet it was something more than this. In retrospect, it was not just that geographical and social spaces opened up, but it was as if society had succumbed to an intoxication with space and time.

The intoxication with time resulted first of all from the directly perceptible increase in speed, hastened and mediated by technology, but absorbed into the life of society as a whole, an increase which individuals could not evade. Technological change means nothing other than the accelerated sequence of social changes. The speed with which a good deal of social distance was reduced, and how quickly habits could change or a good deal of social distance could shrink, caused people to overlook to begin with how little other, invariable power structures were changing. Only from today's standpoint does it become clear that technologies do not always bring the promised liberation, but that they definitely can be used to perpetuate existing inequalities.

The intoxication with speed came to Europe from the United States after a time-lag. There was hardly an account of a journey from the twenties and thirties by Europeans who had returned from the USA which was not fascinated by the hectic pace prevailing there and the cult of speed, commented on by the Europeans with a mixture of admiration and the forebodings of cultural pessimism. Quite a few practitioners of the new psychology were confronted in their analytical sessions with the anxiety and the neuroses of those of their patients who could not cope with the temporal demands. A kind of 'cultural hypochondria' broke out, which gave warning of the disastrous consequences of the intoxication with speed and causally connected many ills of the period with it.[11] Conversely, it was this very cult of speed which was emphatically celebrated in the futurist manifesto. The dynamics of the machine age, as the futurists saw it, was energy translated into speed up to the final consequences of self-destruction – war.

The other form of the intoxication with time consisted in the discovery of world-wide simultaneity. It feigned a sense of time according to which the individual could be in any place at the same time and participate in everything happening elsewhere. The present was everywhere, and one could communicate with people all over the place. And what was to be communicated was the fact that the thirst for knowledge about what was happening elsewhere, for information about other places, other events, other people, was not yet threatened with permanent oversatiation as it is today. In their own way, the writers of *poésie simultanée*, like Apollinaire and others, gave expression to what was expected of simultaneity by a generation which was not yet suffering from the shortage of time that prevails today, nor yet had to indulge in desperate efforts to find time for love as well in an overcrowded appointments diary. Even though it was an artistic avant-garde which thought it could blithely shrug off constraints of space and time, and celebrated what Western, individualized consciousness was bold enough to celebrate for the first time – namely the fundamental experience that the subjectivity of private existence was a reality – many other people shared this experience with them. The bourgeois individual, and this is what we are talking about here, who had also been repeatedly circumscribed by the prevailing social order, was suddenly confirmed in his or her very own, subjective experience through the use of pieces of technological equipment which allowed him or her to establish a link of simultaneity with other individuals in other places. Accordingly, the sum total of all private existences constituted a spatially permissible diversity of reality. What positively exploded through the discovery of simultaneity was the temporal objectivization and legitimation of the individual consciousness, of the subjectively experienced existence. From then on, there was not just one historical 'world-time', analysed and thought out further by Voltaire and other thinkers since the Enlightenment; its disintegration into something that was a kind of co-presences was comprehensible to subjective existences which were objectivized because technologically linked with one another and constituting public time. There were as many subjective times as there were thinking, feeling, knowing, communicating individuals. Thus the bourgeois individual discovered his or her own temporal subjectivity against the background of a growing international integration by means of transport systems and business relations, unwillingly represented by the artistic avant-garde. This temporal subjectivity could be interpreted as a component of public time because private time was thenceforth to be recognized as legitimate, or as a preliminary form of the resistance to those impersonally exercised constraints of time which were already inherent in the technological and economic forms of organization. In the supposed simultaneity, the objective existence of which seemed indubitable owing to its technological embodiment, there was room for one's own subjectivity, it was part of the objective spatio-temporal reality; but it could already – legitimately – be conceived as contrasting with and opposed to it.

Today – fifty and more years, as well as a world war, later – a recurring discovery of simultaneity can be detected. There is no lack of protagonists seeking to celebrate each latest generation of telecommunication technologies as a 'revolution' and promising a fresh liberation of human beings through the merging of space and time, of workplace, working hours, free time and home. In contrast to the beginning of this century, however, when millions of people noted with astonishment the marvels of technology, which immensely stimulated their imagination but only gradually impinged on their own lives, today almost everyone has become involved or at least potentially affected. What was then reserved for a few privileged people has risen, in industrialized countries at least, to a general standard. In the USA in the last ten years alone the share of investments by firms in the purchase of information technologies like computers, tele-communications systems and equipment has doubled from 20 to 40 per cent, as the Office of Technology Assessment notes in its report on the situation of American industry.[12] Other countries are following suit at appropriate intervals. In the Third World, coups d'état have been prepared with the aid of transistor radios, and the television aerials on the tin roofs of slums have become proverbial. The global village of which one of the early enthusiasts of the approaching age of information, Marshall McLuhan, wrote as early as the sixties, in which there would be no shortage of possibilities of communication, seems to have been turned into a reality.

But there is not only joy and jubilation about the new simultaneity. The social repercussions of the new information technologies are at the centre of heated public debates, which spark off questions of property rights and public control, economic concentration and the protection of citizens against unauthorized linking of data gathered about them. Above all, however, the unemployment figures in the industrial nations and the assumed causal nexus with the 'job-destroying' potential of the new technology cast a shadow over the elation. The restraint of state monopolies over institutions of communication and information, and questions of what kind of infrastructure, pricing policy, consumer and data protection to invest in, are merely a few main features of an area of politics which has grown in a subtly diversified way, and the existence of which the advocates of *poésie simultanée* would never have thought possible. The initially celebrated experience of privateness as a legitimate part of a publicly recognized simultaneity has turned into real nightmares of the vulnerability of the private sphere, which has to take refuge from the excess of what is technologically possible in new basic rights and other protective legislation. The variety introduced into the daily routine of steady habits by the first radio programmes and the incipient leisure industry has given way to a surplus of aims and styles of leisure. Despite a reduction of the working week, the journeys to work and journey times are getting longer, and the social costs of any kind of mobility higher. Despite being incomparably better equipped with mechanical household appliances, women still do more housework than men, and they are left with less work-free time in the almost constant ratio of 1:3.[13] Increased standards of cleanliness, longer journey times, even to take children to school or to their leisure activities, dealing with authorities and other public institutions, and finally holiday stress and all the unfinished things which have become the paraphernalia of the modern individual permanently suffering from lack of time, no longer admit the sense of leisure. Simultaneity has everyone under control. Spans of attention have been scientifically investigated and are used for the efficient structuring of commercials on television. What passes over the screen in colourful succession is a parody of simultaneity: the events which are shown follow the rules of dramatic portrayal by a medium. They have little to do with the social reality from which they have been detached. Whether they are fiction or are to be seen from the point of view of simultaneity has become largely irrelevant to the observer.

What was euphorically celebrated at the turn of the century has become prosaic reality today, but with nontrivial consequences. The plurality of private time forces its way into publicity, is absorbed by it. From the original experience of private time and subjectively justified temporal existence, the temporal self, and also the bourgeois one, has been catapulted into working-time regulations, lifetime regulations, retirement age regulations. The private time of every man and woman has found its place, its time, in world time, but through communication technologies this private time has become one which is always connectable, available, and public. In between there lies a process of the collective appropriation of communication technologies which matured technologically after the Second World War. Through the creation of a corresponding infrastructure and that typical convergence of individual technological systems into a gigantic techno-system, in which the diverse sectors are combined with one another,[14] the technological and economic preconditions have been created to make communicating and acting in an approximative simultaneity not just possible, but a necessity. Simultaneity has become workaday routine for many people. It is no longer predominantly dramatic events, like the fate of the sinking *Titanic* or those ritual moments which serve to strengthen the feeling of solidarity among people, which convey simultaneity, but the course of everyday work, the constant temporal presence, real or virtual, of others.

There were social techniques of producing simultaneity in other centuries too, of course, above all the elaborated technique of the ritual which was developed by people in all cultures. In its social orchestration, this was also intent on establishing relations with the natural and supernatural environment and incorporating the existing social order into its coding. In the ritual, spaces and times could be effortlessly overcome, as it were. But it was the proper time of the group which took precedence over the proper time of the individual. It was the group which produced time in the ritual, rehearsed it, caused it to flow into

other temporal transitions, and finally dissolved it. It was
systems of order which had been made by others that were
confirmed in the ritual by the participants, but there was
as yet no individually detachable form of mediation which
could be bought on the market. What the mediation of the
sense of simultaneity by modern technologies and that by
the old social techniques have in common is the social
obligation to join in. Anyone who does not participate
remains outside, becomes an outsider. Only the obligation
to join in has now become an economically mediated one.
The steep social hierarchies which still prevailed at the
turn of the century may have been dismantled in favour of
a middle class which has grown in numbers, but social
inequalities have not disappeared. They can be translated
into temporal inequalities. Society runs the risk of moving
at two speeds, as they say in France, *à deux vitesses*. The
fast group are doing it right. They are, from a technological point of view, up to date, ahead of the competition.
They are rewarded for it, in material terms as well. The
slow group are far from being socially recognized in their
slowness. It requires poetic imagination to portray a world
in which both, the fast and the slow group, have their
complementary place. The author Sten Nadolny has
turned his *Entwicklungsroman** about the English seafarer
and North Pole explorer John Franklin into a subtle study
of the art of being slow and giving meaning to the rhythm
of life. In his days as a ship's captain, the hero records in
his diary: 'The slow job is the more important one. All the
normal, quick decisions are taken by the First Officer.'
In addition, he ponders on the discovery of his friend
Dr Orme, who suggested, in view of the 'fatal acceleration
of the age', measuring the speed of all individuals with
instruments and then deciding what each one was particularly suited to. There are 'overview occupations', like coach-
man or Member of Parliament, and 'detail occupations'

---

* A novel showing the development of a character. (Tr.)

like craftwork or the medical profession or painting. Those in the former can well be exposed to the acceleration of the age; those in the latter will be best able to follow it from their seclusion and carefully judge the work of the fast group and the rulers from its results.[15]

The slow group are those who have been socially left behind. In an interview with an unemployed youth, which was recorded in February 1984 in Bremen in the course of an empirical investigation, the 'standstill' of time in the social situation of being 'unemployed' is made plain. 'Tiger', as the youth calls himself, wants to make time stand still because 'there must not be such a bad time in his life'. His strategies are directed towards making this time irrelevant. But far more than this becomes apparent. A standstill means a relapse in time. Tiger and his family – his father is a dockworker – live in a temporally different, in an anachronistic world. With their needs, their sacrifices, indeed even in the way they practise solidarity, they lag behind the 'historical' time of their social environment. The connection of a telephone becomes the symbol of their 'connection' with the outside world. The family comes under this pressure, however, only through the father's illness and the drama of a possible 'too late'.[16]

Simultaneity, which we are also talking about here in its absence, does not automatically become translatable into equality. In this respect it is an illusion, just as it is clear that within the world of physics there can be no simultaneity. In contrast to the bold promise of one commentator at the turn of the century, space and time have not been annihilated. The convergence mediated by simultaneity via obligations to join in built into technologies and the techno-system gives inequality an additional temporal dimension. This appears not least in the situation in which many developing countries find themselves today. The progress of humanity conceived in evolutionary terms still compares itself with the arrow of time which points irreversibly forwards. For a long time, the various stages of development which societies supposedly had to pass through suggested that there could be only one evolutionary ladder. In the meantime, the paths have become more winding, and the all too simplistic thought patterns have been discredited. Measured against the degree of implementation of technologies and their concentration, the contours of the temporal differences stand out more sharply. In the old evolutionary ladder of social development, shaped by European ethnocentrism, the hierarchically temporal conception of different speeds of development also had a – patriarchal – protective function: the less developed societies were acknowledged to live in a different time, and their officially declared backwardness allowed them to some extent to retain their own lifestyle. Living at the end of the civilized world was equated with a certain right to temporal backwardness. Being exposed to the pressure of simultaneity, as occurs in view of the thrust towards development by modern telecommunications technologies, means forfeiting the right to one's own speed of development. What counts is no longer the ideological justification, but the temporal-technological obligation to join in. In view of the illusion of simultaneity, it becomes even more difficult to refuse the programme of a development intent on catching up – the patterns of perception have been changed too much by the technological possibilities, and the dependences relating to financial policy are too real, which, via the temporal apparatus of the credit system, map out the path to come.[17]

If anthropologists criticize their own discipline by saying that in their fieldwork, in conversation with their informants, its practitioners acknowledge to their opposite number that the 'other' is located in the same time as the anthropologists, since only on this condition is communication possible, while the same anthropologists, in writing scientific texts, constitute the 'other' as an object who lives in another time, the time of 'tribal reality' – then this shows another problematic aspect of simultaneity.[18] The existence of different and contradictory forms of consciousness in the same time, their temporal co-presence, can be denied, or established as distance. 'Distance is something the forces of progress need so that it can be overcome with time.' But can all dating in an imaginary or conventional chronology of development be avoided by recognizing temporal co-presence, even if this chronology is not conceived in deterministic and evolutionary terms? Is the village scribe whom Jean-Jacques Salomon comes across in the French central Alps when he is preparing to write his book about the computer age an anachronism, or is his existence part of the everyday juxtaposition of times, even in a state which prides itself on its high technology?[19] Is the unemployed 20-year-old 'Tiger' temporally less 'behind' if as an interview partner he is recognized in his spatio-temporal presence as co-temporal, as a contemporary? Who is making what ascriptions here, and how do things stand in social reality – really?

It is certainly correct that the distances from the respective 'others' in the developmental history of humanity have shrunk, and that precisely in the shifting of the balance between 'I' and 'we' there also lies an element of the process of civilization.[20] Denying the 'other' a soul and hence humanity, or shunting him or her on to a lower stage of development, classifying him or her in another time, admittedly express various forms of distancing, but still always remain social distancing and hence an invitation to discrimination. In Western industrial societies, the unemployed live in a different time. It may be the temporal 'moratorium' which 'Tiger' imposes on himself, or it may be the agonizingly slow passing of time described by Marie Jahoda in her classic study on the unemployed of Marienthal, where a whole morning's activity is summed up in the statement 'meanwhile it's getting on for lunchtime'.[21] But do the unemployed live in a different time because they are or were not fast enough, or are they unable to be fast enough because they are unemployed?

What is juxtaposition of times in view of a situation of temporal co-presence here, and what – intentional or un-intentional – togetherness? How can the indisputable fact of the different speeds in the courses of time, measured against a normative target of temporal development, be revoked, whose imperative is derived from the illusion of simultaneity?

In physics, thanks to the accuracy attained in the measurement of time, the predictions of the Special Theory of Relativity have been directly observed. If two observers are equipped with clocks and move at constant speed relatively to one another, the clock of the one or other will be slow in comparison. The concept of simultaneity for two events occurring in different places has thus lost its significance in terms of physics. Each observer has his or her 'proper' time, which is measured by an accurate clock and which is always borne with him or her. If all the relative speeds of the different observers are known, their proper time can be calculated by means of the mathematical equations of the theory.

In social life there is also a proper time which everybody bears with them. It arose relatively late, and its capacity for political articulation is only in the process of development. In earlier societies there were hardly signs, and there was also no need, of an individualized time. The social time of the group, of the tribe, held good for all members, even though distinctions grew along the lines of social distinction: according to sex, according to age-groups, according to occupation based on the division of labour, according to status and according to power. The European Middle Ages, which lived largely without clocks, developed different systems of time for different social activities. The religious sphere – as in other social systems – was an exception, and also held a special position with regard to time. Not only were there 'holy times', the set times in the flow of secular time, but work in the 'service of God', as the religious sector was called, followed its own strict temporal rules. The conflict over time first flared up when God's time was no longer consistent with that of traders, and it became unclear whether it was permitted to lend money in order to earn interest in time.[22]

The endless quarrels over the reform of the Gregorian Calendar and over the standardization of local times which differed from town to town were conflicts over the territorial scope of certain social systems each of which had its corresponding system of time. For the people who lived in these systems, however, it was their occupation, their status, and their place of residence that decided which rules of time they had to follow. With the advent of clocks, communally usable, visible reference points were created, which were superior in accuracy and reliability to the means of orientation previously used, the observation of heavenly bodies or the behaviour of animals. It was enough now to glance up at the clock on the church steeple to find out what time it was. One's own sense of time, regulated by the recurring festivals of the ecclesiastical year, by social habits and the necessity of adapting one's work rhythm to the requirements of agriculture, was sufficient to dictate the generally valid, social time. Only with the advent of capitalism, when time could be converted into money, did the attitude towards time characteristic of industrial societies emerge, and the process of detachment of a lifetime which had become measurable in working hours begin. The machine first required to be operated – to the point of total exhaustion. The time that was left was used up in restoring the capacity for work which had been expended in one's working hours. The relation of one's own time to that of others, to social time, had come under the laws of economy – the economy of time. The machine dictated the metronomic rhythm for the machine age. Viewed in this light, the struggle of the organized labour movement in the nineteenth century for shorter working hours was a first step towards the recognition of a minimal proper time, but this was still viewed wholly as collective time and filled with contents which had been collectively mapped out: those of urgently needed recuperation. For the bourgeois individual, however, the emergence of individuality and subjectivity brought a separate sense of time. But the latter remained, as for the female reader of the novel, or for entries in the diary, which became the temporal organ of private feelings, still wholly embedded in the private sphere, withheld from the eyes of others, the secret time of the emergent self.[23]

Only at the turn of this century, as was shown earlier in this chapter, was there an explosive emergence into public life of these millions of subjective times which had previously been kept secret – prepared by the processes of economic integration, and made possible by the technologies which were capable of creating the illusion of simultaneity. It was the epoch in which proper time was constituted, just as it was the 'saddle period' from 1750 to 1850 which had constituted 'modern times' and the temporalization of history. It was up to an artistic and scientific avant-garde to express its new perceptions, experiences and feelings. It was not just by chance that the psychological theories of the time were intensively concerned with the problem of perception, of duration, of memory and of the traces which every temporal perception left behind in the memory. It was not by chance that the Theory of Relativity, even though it was understood by scarcely more than a handful of physicists, met with an enormous popular scientific response. It was not by chance that the fascination of simultaneity, precisely because it still represented the extraordinary, extended to the smallest village, even though the only evidence of this is what historians have found in the oral historical tradition. The emergence of proper time, in its subjectively experienced quality and scientifically grounded for the first time, thus entered the public domain. But it needed a further, social-organizational and technological infrastructure, created only in the second half of this century, to socialize proper time, to practise its use, and to make it a habit which has since made its temporal mark on everyday life. Here it is now practised and experienced, and in cases of conflict also suffered. Here it is trivialized. Since the socialized version of proper time, its now public dissemination and acquisition by everyone, just like the subjectivized version before it, the articulation of which was reserved for a minority, is mediated via technology, it seems reasonable to look for the determinants of the temporal changes in technology itself. It was as true then as it is today that 'cultural hypochondria' is never very far away from what is regarded as a non-pathological normal state. Numerous fears and prognoses arise in connection with the widespread invasion by telecommunications media of all spheres of social existence. They warn of the dangers of a possible psychological isolation, a social uncoupling in a hyper-individualized world of one's own. Temporal perceptions, mediated via the screen, can lead to extreme fragmentation even in the perception of social relations. Sherry Turkle describes the psycho-structure of young computer freaks who, through interaction with technology, create their own world – even in terms of time – which largely isolates them from the social events around them.[24] Maruyama reports on a new generation of Japanese youths whom, following the computer generations, he calls the fifth generation of computer kids. They are developing hitherto unknown cognitive faculties which are lacking in the older generation, even if the latter has already grown up with computers. Thus, among other things, they are able to see several programmes on video screens simultaneously, and to grasp the narrative structures; they develop their own games whose rules provide for a continuous switching on and switching off, and patterns of temporal perception combining speed and simultaneity.[25]

But technologies alone can never manufacture time, any more than clocks, which indicate time. This requires interaction between people, from which mechanisms of coordination arise, functionally instrumental, but which are also used as symbolic means of orientation. Technologies mediate in these processes, channel, guide, give directions, and tend to alleviate or aggravate, increase or reduce social differences and distances between people. But they are not the 'neutral tool' they are still often portrayed to be. Such a point of view denies the history of every technology, its derivation from previous generations of technology and their social origins and foundations. Michael Young views social evolution as essentially driven forward by the evolution of tools, parallel to biological evolution, which have developed into external organs of human beings. Like Leroi-Gourhan before him, he stresses the extra-somatic character of technological evolution by means of tools, which above all results in the range and capabilities of human sense organs being increased. By means of technological tools and equipment, the human eye can see, and the ear can hear, things which remain closed to it by nature. Information technologies, and especially the computer, are similarly beginning to increase and to amplify the capabilities of the human brain far beyond present achievements. The tools and machines with which human beings have surrounded themselves are being incorporated by them again in a certain sense. Society is assimilating its technologies again, they are becoming a habit, a habitualized way of life which leads to further use of the external sense organs. Like all habits, they soon become a matter of course; the habit of machinery then blends with the biological and social rhythms. 'A tool of any complexity', writes Michael Young, 'is a kind of material habit which encapsulates in the present the past experience of countless generations, and which is further elaborated before being handed on in a modified form, to be discarded or modified again.'[26]

The process of habituation to the new technologies is still in full swing. It is always also a learning and mastering process. What the machinery has to offer – global simultaneity and the social representation and integration into it of countless, local proper times – is being rehearsed at the moment, and turned into social habituation. Through technology, people's relations with one another change, but a new relationship between proper time and the social time which unites people can also be established through it. There is a long way to go, however. At the moment, the juxtaposition of times outweighs a new togetherness. The struggle for the social recognition of proper time and its representation in the global, standardized system of world time as a political fact, too, began with the spread of the technological infrastructure and the obligations to join in produced by it. It is being continued by the struggle for a political structuring of the structuring spaces and times thus opened up. This makes it clear why the aspect of conflict in habituation is so strongly to the fore at present. Proper time, viewed as self-time from the perspective of the individual, has to come to fresh terms with the time of others, with outside time, above all in the institutionalized complex of working hours and its changed relations to time free of work. It also becomes clear why it is not so much psychology or physics which lie at the heart of the challenge, in the scientific observation and in the first phase of the subjective grounding of proper time, but rather biology and sociology, and certainly also political science. For in order to find a fairly acceptable social 'solution' to the need for coordination of proper times, the proper time which people bear within them as biological beings in their common features, but also in their individual variations, must be considered in the rules of social existence and of technological mediation. The solution presupposes that the 'specious present' is not just interpreted as a phenomenon of individual psychology, but becomes socially and politically interpretable.

It also becomes clear why the structuring of proper time is confronted with two problems which are to be settled in the life of every individual and at the level of society. They are linked by what has here been described as the juxtaposition of times: out of the awareness, already put forward as a problem, of the temporal co-presence of proper times, which is technologically held together and yet temporally differentiated by the illusion and the norm of simultaneity. This requires an examination of the resultant tendencies socially to tolerate, indeed to sanction social inequalities as non-simultaneities. The small temporal difference, which becomes ever larger in its social repercussions, driven forward by international economic and technological competition, leads to the danger that the juxtaposition of courses of time and different speeds results in social divisions, and that large sections of the population are temporally left behind. How much temporal drifting apart a society can bear, and whether acceleration can be made controllable, consciously slowed down or delayed, is an open question arising from the juxtaposition of proper times, which not only concerns norms of social justice but is also important, as shown in the next chapter, for economic and technological development. The other complex of questions results from the point of view of the temporalization of proper times themselves. For every individual proper time has its history. It begins in childhood and with that which is further learnt about society; it changes, in keeping with social circumstances, into old age and up until death. One's own biography, in which the irreversible arrow of time is incorporated, consists of the combination of sequences. Only thus is social identity constituted and changed. Through the juxtaposition of times in a highly differentiated society, the individual is also faced with very different temporal pressures, to reconcile proper time with the requirements of institutionalized outside time; pressures and expectations which can vary greatly in temporal terms in the course of one's biography. Arranging sequences means being able to produce meaningful relations between them and thereby establishing identity. Juxtaposition can also occur in one's own life

– it is then necessary, according to Luhmann, at least to retain one's sensitivity to coincidence, for this is what can still lend continuity to the gathering of coincidences.[27]

Individual proper time is necessarily fitted into the length of a lifetime. Longer periods of experience are open to society; even if, as the core of the systematic reflection of historiography requires, it arranges sequences, and gives them meaning, to rearrange them again in the light of later, fresh experiences, the various modalities in which people's experiences produce history are still 'stratified', in a temporally graduated fashion. Simultaneity has already been treated here, and it recurs in the form of the 'possibility of narrating the experiences of those involved', as the historian Reinhart Koselleck believes. He focuses on various ways of gaining experience. The first kind of experience is always as unique as it is unrepeatable. It is the experience which is the result of surprise, since 'somebody has an experience who has to be surprised'. Hence it also has to be repeatedly undergone afresh by every single person. What is repeated is simply this fact. The second possibility of gaining experience is that which is repeated, whether in the life of a single person, or as the result of a process of accumulation, and hence through the experience of many people. Experience is stabilized in the medium term here, and experiences are specific to one's generation to an increased extent. They result from the biological handicap alone, which moulds every individual life through the temporal discrepancy between parents and children, but they receive their social signature through the political and social events experienced in common, as a generation. Although they are differently perceived and undergone, such phases of experience nevertheless evoke a minimum of common interests, comprehending all age-groups. Once these are institutionalized, they establish a common history.

To these two interlinked and mutually interdependent levels of time – the unique level and that conditioned by one's generation – a third level can be added, that which in the long term, whether insidiously or in phases, alters all established experiences, and changes the balance of experience altogether. Such long-term historical changes, which influence every current conflict or help to cause it, remain present as a background experience, even if they are raised into consciousness only by questions of historical method.

But just as the individually experienced biography must be repeatedly restructured to produce a continuous narrative, room must also be made in history for the experiences of succeeding generations. Here, at the latest, proper time meets history: 'Whatever is mustered, especially in the way of statistical methods, it continues to be a question of finding long-term changes or lasting assumptions in order to be able to comprehend the uniqueness of one's own surprise.'[28] Surprise indicates that the time-curve of history cannot simply be extrapolated from the past, that there can be discontinuities and breaks. The approximative simultaneity which this century, with the aid of its technologies, has made a reality and used as an illusion may certainly represent a surprise, in the sense of having to have an experience. As such, it deserves to be included in the process of writing down, extrapolating and rewriting history.

2

From the Future to the Extended Present

A horizon is nothing, save the limit of your sight.

John Donne

With the Enlightenment, there also arose the need for time; for it was necessary to make up the delay of reason. There was only one means of making it up, that of speeding up proceedings. This is how Hans Blumenberg describes the central ideas of an age which first discovered progress and commandeered it for itself, and to which the consumption of time appeared a quantity that could be controlled. The idea of speeding up was still wholly tied to the agonizing thought of the 'delay of reason', but already oriented itself to the notion of the consumption of time for the historical achievement which was still to be performed. 'Time, until then merely the medium for the appearance of events and protagonists, for the growth of subliminal empirical quantities into measurable results, itself becomes a power which can be thought capable of anything by virtue of its sheer quantity.'[1] Everything seemed possible, if only it had time enough, it would be said later. To begin with, the need was concentrated on gaining time, on the process of catching up which drew on the past. The horizon of time was powerfully shifted back in this direction, to begin with; biblical chronology was provincialized. 'Room is made in the space of time for the great extra-biblical cultures and for the supposedly long-term processes of the moral and rational perfection of human beings.' But it was obvious that the need for time also had to spread to the future, since the present could hardly be regarded as the perfection of all things. Problems of consciousness thereby arose for the individual which 'were to tear the latter to and fro between encouragement and despair in the face of a conception of history of such spaciousness that the individual life seemed to have no significance in it any longer.'[2] As an answer to the need for time which had become apparent, however, the attribution of meaning had to keep pace with the change of temporal perspectives, the extension into the past and into the future at the same time. The past could 'extend to genuine or false infinity', the illusion of closely centred conceptions of history could be destroyed and replaced by a world history of the human race. But for the future, it could neither be denied nor repressed that the lifetime still remained the measure of meaningful life expectancy.

> Every extension of progress beyond what was still attainable by the present and individual consciousness endangered the structure of meaning which guaranteed the intended share of the individual in the continuance of the whole . . . Speeding up under the idea of 'progress' could and would not just mean securing its inner logic and making it irreversible, but also retrieving an indefinitely open future and putting it into lifetime proportions. Or at least supplying the extent of the individual lifetime with as many future possibilities as are attainable. The future dimension of progress should thus be anything but the temporal counterpart of the past whose dimensions are newly discovered and still to be discovered . . . In the tension which arose through the dissociation of lifetime and world time, it amounted to drawing or forcing more and ultimately perhaps everything into the life expectancy of the concrete and frail subject. Therefore 'progress' becomes something which does not just spring from its inevitability as regards objective content . . . , but which can be advanced by method, organization and institution, and condensed by speeding it up.[3]

The eighteenth century, Blumenberg concludes, did not yet believe that human beings make history, but what could be made was the pace of history: 'Stepping up the pace presupposes the inevitability, safeguarded elsewhere, of the sequences. Not an edifying result; but, recognizable by its fascination, apparently the most comforting one in the face of the temporal dimension of the future.'[4] In the nineteenth century, human beings made history – as Karl Marx correctly recognized – and by means of machines. The speeding up of the 'formal outline' had found its unsurpassed method and form of organization in the machine geared to industrial production. The newly invented 'economy of time, in which all time becomes economy' consisted in the fact that more was produced within the same time unit, or the same volume could be produced within a shorter time unit.[5] The speeding up by the machine was oriented to a different, mobile continuum of reference which had become the symbol of the machine age or, in Lewis Mumford's phrase, the key machine of the industrial age per se: the clock. The 'inevitability, safeguarded elsewhere, of the sequences', which could be fed into the rhythm of the machines, first of all forced people who had to work at them to adapt themselves to standards of performance which were becoming quicker and quicker. When English industrial workers smashed the clock mounted above the factory entrance (and not the machines at which they worked), their anger was directed at the hated symbol of timekeeping, by means of which their accelerated output was monitored.[6] Finally, in Taylorism* there followed the almost complete equation of an organic series of movements with the series of movements performed by machines, both prescribed in their inevitable sequences and measured by clock time. In the idea that all reserves of

* A reference to the doctrine of the American engineer Frederick Winslow Taylor (1856–1915), the founder of 'scientific management'. (Tr.)

time, however insignificant they appeared, the hidden
pauses and slow-downs, were to be 'rationalized away',
the speeding up that was attainable by 'method, organization and institution' reached its provisional peak. What
was to be forced into the lifetime of the 'concrete and frail
subject' had indeed been pressed into it.

The open horizon of the future, however, which just like
the expanded past was indebted to the need for time felt
by the Enlightenment and became an integral part of the
belief in progress, was able to stabilize as the difference,
permanently to be sustained, between experience already
undergone and the horizon of expectation. The traditional
space of experience and the horizon of expectation –
previously – derived from it diverged; in the concept of
progress this increasing distinction was repeated. Because
the horizon of expectation was set in motion, history
was made dynamic. As Koselleck strikingly proves, the
modern era of history, which could now be explicitly
called such, and its progress, became applicable in the
same sense. Through changes in quick succession, which
were experienced first as unique, and then as supersedable
experiences of reality, the space of experience changed. At
the same time, however, that expectation increased which
was directed towards the open horizon of the future and
promised a constant opening up into something better.[7]

This difference had continuously to be sustained. While
it was constitutive for so long for the belief in progress, it
did not last in the end – either in the precarious balance
between world time and lifetime, or as the collectively
keepable promise of a constant, glorious improvement of
the future. The open horizon in terms of world history has
repeatedly darkened, and at the moment the cloud of
further, man-made catastrophes is hanging heavily over it.
Viewed in terms of the lifetime, progress has admittedly
brought a catching up in social prosperity and material
well-being for many people, in the industrialized countries
at least. But individual happiness, multiplied by the large

number of all those who also want to enjoy it in the same place and at the same time, is, as a glance at jammed motorways or similar consumer pleasures shows, of relatively brief duration and diminished content. What the future promises in the way of expectations seems to be at best more of the same and at worst a diminution of stock. Even acceleration does not help any further here. Since having to run faster in order to stay in one and the same spot exposes a different experience of progress, which in a relative state of being ahead can demonstrate an equal state of being behind. The escape routes which are supposed to lead out of the expectation of the future, which has become peculiarly empty, remain ensnared in the same basic pattern. They either point to a non-existent idyllic past or place their hopes in the next phase of technological innovation. But despite predictions and promises, the horizon remains flat and motionless. The dynamics of depth of focus has clearly been lost. Progress itself, it may be said, has aged. In the ecological sphere, the repercussions are the most dramatic, because here linearity – the continuous pushing out on a continuum temporally directed towards the future – has most drastically and most lastingly turned out to be an unfounded hope. In the biosphere as in the geosphere it is sudden events instead, the 'upsetting' of natural balances, and the effects arising from synthetic reactions, which from the combination of processes of different kinds with mostly unknown proper times can lead to discontinuities and breakdowns.[8] With the reduction of the time-scales within which mostly unpleasant consequences of present or yesterday's actions are to be expected, the pressure of time also grows which weighs heavily on the present. It is not so much the apocalyptically tinged visions of the end of time, but the at least scientifically plausible assumptions of clear periods of time within which negative consequent effects become foreseeable. The future mapped out in linear terms draws dangerously close to the present, filled with conditional negatives. If solutions are to be found which are to be realized as well, then as soon as possible. Now.

Thus it is not just that 'the future is no longer what it used to be', as a piece of graffiti announces from the wall of a house in Berlin. It is increasingly overshadowed by the problems which are opening up in the present. The future no longer offers that projection space into which all desires, hopes and fears could be projected without many inhibitions because it seemed sufficiently remote to be able to absorb everything which had no place or was unwelcome in the present. The future has become more realistic, not least because the horizon of planning has been extended. But this also means that it is drawing closer to the present. With the abundance of human activities and their repercussions over a period of time, which become apparent because they require periods of planning and development that cannot be reduced at will and can be cancelled only with difficulty, a momentum of the present has been established which has to concentrate on itself. The scope of action is restricted because a part of the future is already being disposed of in the present; the ecological loops of human action become loops of time which react upon the present. The invocation of the future, in the name of which political action was justified for a long time, had to be reduced and at least partly transferred to the present.

Time conflicts and temporal asymmetries resulting from the need for coordination and integration of different time-structures and structuring patterns can be resolved by institutional mechanisms which establish priorities or invent workable compromises,[9] or they find direct expression in the change of cultural symbols which serve as means of orientation. 'Time', as the Finnish philosopher von Wright concluded in an astute analysis, 'is man's flight from contradiction.'[10] In order to be able to accept change, time has to be created. In order to be able to accept changes with time, it could be continued, the categories of time have to be changed repeatedly. This is happening at present, under the pressure produced by the collapse of the concept of progress and the potentially negative consequent effects, which are becoming manifest with delays in time through the effect on the natural environment. The temporal category of the future is being abolished and replaced by that of the extended present.[11]

The contradiction which is being fled from in this way arises, among other things, from the fact that the insatiable desire for technological and scientific innovations, and the rapid pace at which they are to be converted into economic growth, produce both the unforeseeable element and the essence of the innovation, and in addition also seek to bring under control all the consequent effects of this very innovation. The open horizon is to be preserved, and what has not been conceived is to remain conceivable, yet the positive and negative repercussions are equally to be known and controllable in advance. 'Choosing the future', determining it, so runs a popular political slogan; it suggests that it is in fact possible to choose and determine. Such a demand is intended to open up scope for participatory structuring and to encourage people; to rouse the imagination, which threatens to ossify over the monotony of everyday life and the tightening regulations within and between institutions. A 'different' lifestyle, a 'different' way of working, is to be propagated. But this future which is to be created is already taking place now, is being determined in the extended present.[12]

The fact that the future is being generated in the present, that it is a relatively brief period of time at the beginning of a sequence which determines the further course of processes, is confirmed by analyses dealing with the genesis of technology. Initially, in the case of every innovation there are countless possibilities for development, which very soon undergo a radical limitation, however, in the sense of an evolutionary selection.[13] What is left immediately after the elimination of the competition of a great variety which do not prove to be serviceable is a few options. The time-paths become compressed and narrower. The extended present has chosen the future and not vice versa.

The future is constricted 'in time' by the planning of longer-term intentions. It contains both: the symbolic construct which consists in the shifting of the drawing up of the boundary of time, and the real anticipations made by planning, by decisions about financing, and by action in organization, which are established in the extended present. Because the relation between present and future shifts, the future can be put into operation – in the present. The longer-term interdependences begin to take shape. The limited understanding in the recognition of problems and the equally limited means of mastering them which are available today likewise refer to the period of time lying immediately ahead, and not to a distant future. With the mounting pressure that solutions to impending, recognizable problems have to be found now, and with the ticking of the many clocks which have installed warning signals, there does not remain enough time to accommodate them in a moment conceived as fleeting, or to consign them to the amnesia of the future. The future of our children is no longer predominantly interpreted in individual terms – as the desire for social advancement and well-being – but as a question of collective survival. It is the time of the next generation which is being argued about now. The dramatic increase in complexity and density draws the future closer to the present – not just for the conscientious manager who already enters appointments in next year's calendar. This is also true of the calendar of societies. The years 2000 or 2025 are almost within reach.[14] A loan is raised on a future by the latter being fetched into an extended present, in the hope that the present will suffice to yield the requisite interest – and the added value – needed for repayment. The future is disposed of as if it were the present, and an extended present is thereby produced.

For Emile Durkheim, who wrote *The Elementary Forms of Religious Life* in 1912, it was obvious that it was the forms of social organization from which people draw their fundamental thought categories such as space and time. For a 'conception' of time means nothing other than an intellectual grasp of that which surrounds people in their natural and social environment. And Norbert Elias stresses:

> that time assumes the character of a universal dimension, is nothing other than a symbolic expression of the experience that everything which exists is part of a continual sequence of events. Time is an expression of the fact that people seek to determine positions, the length of intervals, the speed of change and more besides in this flow with a view to their own orientation.[15]

It follows from this that, depending on the state of social development, time as a social institution, as a symbolic means of orientation, is differently conceived, and confirmed and institutionalized by behaviour, social habits and interaction. That is why there are different conceptions of time in societies; they change with the demands which are made in the present on the society of individuals.

Yet this is no longer the simple formula of the different evaluation befitting the past, present or future in a society, which was believed not that long ago by empirically oriented social researchers to contain the key to the understanding of problems of time.[16] But the abolition of the category of the future, and its replacement by that of the extended present, does not suffice to cope with all the contradictions which have arisen and the pressure of problems. What has been set in motion is rather also the relationship between the linear and the cyclical conception of time. This is generally regarded as fundamental to the 'temporal architecture of a civilization' (Krzysztof Pomian). Its components can be taken apart and put together again, but even through the plurality of times – psychological time, solar, liturgical and political time, clock time and the ultra-long or extremely brief time of science[17] – the deeply rooted dualism of thought and temporal perception runs in straight lines or in recurring movements. One's own experience of life sufficiently nurtures both views. The movement from birth to death can be conceived as part of a cycle, indeed as recurrence, or as a more or less straight line which runs from the starting point to the final point. The linear, says Michael Young, stresses the new and leaves behind it what is familiar and has already been experienced. Viewed in these terms, it does not repeat itself and nothing is re-peated in it. But no more can the cyclical bring back what is familiar, what has already existed, and what is identical in human life, although it produces something new.[18] As with every dualism, there is ample illustrative material for both ways of seeing things, but in the valuation befitting them from a social standpoint they remain in a peculiarly ambivalent, and unstable, because easily 'revaluable' position. The extended present, which can no longer be conceived in a linearly open, continual future, must therefore necessarily re-evaluate and absorb the body of cyclical time. The arrow of time admittedly continues to point forward, but it is now composed of many, recurring cycles. Science confirms this, as if its report had been ordered by society at the right time. From chronobiology, which deals with circadian rhythms and investigates the different oscillations and frequencies of the cycles of the human organism, via physics to the history of art or economics, science offers a whole host of insights based on a complementary view between the linearity and the cyclicality of time.

If in the life of society, however, the impression prevails that linearity takes precedence over the cyclical conception of time, and if society is furnished with the adjective 'metronomic', there are understandable reasons for this. The contrast between the two fundamental conceptions of time arose with industrialization and the importance given to linear quantification during this period. The clock, although it is itself a measuring instrument geared to periodic recurrence, became the metronome for a changed rhythm of social time.[19] The machines in the factory buildings, although they too were constructed with a periodic recurrence of their mechanical sequences in mind, were rightly regarded as the embodiment of the linearity which was built into the capitalist process of accumulation. It was based on another quantifiable medium, the universal medium of exchange per se, into which time could be transformed from now on: money. Time became money, and more or less money could be made from time. Time could be 'rationalized' from now on, i.e. by the appropriate organization of capital and work, 'saved', 'gained' and 'increased', in order to produce more. Counting hours or minutes, and measuring time, was given an additional instrumental importance with industrialization, which it has not lost to this day.

The measurement of time itself is an ancient cultural phenomenon. Having as biological beings the internal clock within them and the regularly recurring motions of the sun and stars around them, human beings produced a system of measuring time as a cultural achievement early on, which served to orient and coordinate their activities. In agrarian societies, it seemed obvious also to orient oneself in the measurement of time by the course of the cyclically recurring seasons. Over and above the practical functions of coordination, the measurement of time was always also used to project one's own social order and its periods of time into the cosmos and into nature, in order then to elevate the heavenly and natural order to the normative yardstick for the social system of structuring time. The power of the priests resulted from their knowledge and their function as time-givers. The measurement of time consequently serves as a setting of temporal standards and standardizations, from fixing the 'right' moment in the harmony between cosmos and human beings and separating 'sacred' times from profane ones, to the setting of records in sporting competition or the ascertaining of only just perceptible spans of attention for the purposes of conveying information. What has changed is the scales of measurement and instruments. The measurement itself is made by bringing into relation mobile continua which can be of many different kinds, one of which serves as a reference point for the other.[20] In other cultures there was an astonishing abundance of different scales of measurement which served as a reference point, and accordingly many kinds of temporal dimension were measured. Only the scientific measurement of time brought the reduction to a single dimension, the homogenized, linear time of physics.

Socially prevailing notions of time are therefore strongly influenced by the scales of measurement used. The linearized, homogenized continuum of mobile sequences which became the basis of the scientific measurement of time does not remain confined to physics, however. All other processes of measurement return to it. It is built into machines and technological equipment, and it is linked with the idea of measurement per se. And a great deal is measured: from the number of votes cast to the gross national product, from events recorded in the *Guinness Book of Records* to detailed budget expenditure. The idea of a linearized and homogenized scale of measurement has also seized hold of history. Its chronology is regarded as the final authoritative reference point for the course of all events in the human calendar per se. In his critique of chronological time, Siegfried Kracauer attributes the uncritical acceptance enjoyed, in his view, by the conception of flowing time among historians to an irresistible desire to translate the formal quality of irreversible flowing into content. It is the desire to be able to grasp the historical process as a whole, in order to be able to ascribe particular qualities to it as a whole. These may consist in the development of inherent possibilities, or in the idea of progress in the direction of a better future. Neither Hegel nor the comparatively more realistic Marx, nor many others, were able to resist the temptation to try to unfold, tackle and conceive the course of history in its entirety. Chronology is thereby given a 'material' importance of the first order.[21] But the time of the calendar is an empty time, a vessel with no contents.

The mobile continua which are brought into relation with one another in the measurement of time by one serving as a reference point for the other, no matter whether they serve mere dating, dividing up into periods or interpretation, are not chosen arbitrarily, however. They are 'superior' in a very definite sense, and they are made 'superior' relative to the social organization of a society, its power structure, its value system and its built-in dynamics of development. Significances are ascribed to them which, viewed from a different perspective, are not peculiar to them. But once they have attained a significance, this continues to have an effect and rubs off on other interpretations. This was the case in the relation between linearity and cyclicality. Just as the arrow of time which points from the past via the present into the future says nothing as yet about dividing lines which mark individual periods of time, linearity does not rule out a cyclical recurrence from the start. But it is not possible to abstract from human ascriptions of significance. Every conception of time has to accommodate the idea of irreversible change and the idea of repetition; they therefore correspond to the 'reproducible' time of physics. Societies can, however, make a choice within certain limits, construct their time and change this construction again.

For human concerns, it cannot be so easily decided whether the 'closed' past follows a different logic from the always uncertain future and the present which is constantly 'impure' because it can be influenced by human behaviour, systems of belief, and ideas.[22] Even though the past is over, it is capable of stipulating, via long-term historical processes, the marginal conditions within which the present takes place. The future, on the other hand, separable from the present by a fluid dividing line, admittedly promises the wealth of all possibilities and contingencies, but only a limited range of these possibilities can become present reality. The processes of separation are what sociology means by the terms 'structuring' and 'structuration'.[23] Time then becomes in the present 'the possibility of creation and destruction, the source of uncertainty and decision' (Elchardus). It contains the process of becoming, which is removed and also differs in its methodology from the reconstruction of the past. The extended present stresses the necessity of structuring, but also the possibilities of structuring. It tries to diminish the uncertainty of the future by recalling cyclicality and seeking to combine it with linearity. The present is no longer interpreted merely as part of the way on the straight line leading to a future open to progress, but as part of a cyclical movement. In addition, and overlapping with the chronological positioning which becomes a neutral background dating and loses the ideological overloading of a world history with which it was encumbered until recently, events become interpretable as part of a cycle. They are seen as part of a succession, a sequence, which follows its 'own time', which bears within it its clock or – in modern parlance – its programme or its temporal code, which determines ascent, repetition and descent or completion.

It is an astonishing social change which is taking place here. In its shortage of time and embroiled in temporal contradictions, society is using new strategies to try to solve the problematic situations which have emerged. The present is being extended in order to have more time for urgently impending decisions. But it is also being extended in the sense that it is now interpreted both in chronological linear terms and as a part of recurring cycles which all follow their own duration and typical curves of development. Dating now no longer occurs exclusively with reference to the time of the calendar, but with reference to the time of the 'inner programme', the 'genetic code', which dictates the term of one's life. New complementarities are opening up here which are also oriented to the 'proper time' of systems, and for which their positioning in the linear sequence of chronology becomes background noise. Because the ascription of significance shifts to the cycles, to the proper times of the connected events and processes which produce a system, the plurality of times naturally also increases. Many people think the time has come to confront the linearity which has retained predominance even in social life, through industrialization and the ways of life connected with it, deliberately with cyclical time and cyclical ways of life. On this view, their foundations would be discoverable in the biological rhythms of social existence. Habits would give stability to society through their cyclical recurrence. Since they too are subject to social evolution, it is not a static but a dynamic stability which would be produced in this way.[24]

The idea of cyclical recurrence is as old as mythology and the continuation it has found within philosophy. The discovery of cyclical time is not and cannot by any means be new, in view of the fact that cycles are components of natural, cosmological and biological sequences of events. Even the rediscovery of social rhythms could be dismissed as the compensatory longing which fills a society that has grown weary of the domination of the metronome, or could be interpreted as a harmlessly endearing form of conservatism, which seeks to rely on habit as a factor of social stability. But this is not all. Precursors of the idea can be found without much difficulty, and so also can empirical observations. The regularity with which particular forms of economic crisis recurred impressed itself on social science early on. Other phenomena of social life which seemed to recur regularly were also observed, recorded and subjected to statistical analysis: wars, crop failures, revolts, but also seasonal variations in the birth and death rate, in the crime or divorce rate, stimulated the imagination of social science to record more accurate data and to search for the laws concealed in them. Simply on the strength of their far-reaching significance for economic events alone, it was the recurrent economic upturns and downturns which were vigorously examined. A Russian economist, Kondratiev, and after him Schumpeter and many others, thought they had found the pulsating rhythm of recurrence. In the form of so-called long waves, at intervals of about fifty-five years, there are, so runs the hypothesis, phases of technological innovation which have a lasting influence on economic events. Kondratiev himself wrote in 1928 that he was not of the opinion that the periodicity of the natural sciences was commensurate with the social world; by 'regularity' he understood the repetition of particular events or phenomena in time. Since then, with the aid of refined statistical methods and an enlarged data basis, long waves have turned into a small sea of research literature.[25] As it was with Kondratiev himself, it is a question of being able to draw conclusions about the form and length of cycles from the observation of cyclical events, which either recur in strictly periodical fashion or at least show recurring sequences of alternating phases, and of examining their connections with one another.

One person who is examining the discovery of recurring social 'pulses' on the basis of extensive data evidence, and covering a period of 200 years of human inventions, and innovations of a technological and non-technological kind, is the physicist Cesare Marchetti. Radical in his claims, he thinks he has traced the high level of self-organization in Western industrial societies in a quantifiable and hence verifiable form. The kind and number of examples he uses are impressive. It is a question of 'populations' of cars or computers, or of the substitution of each of the most important energy sources, from wood to fusion energy. But a 'population' can also be the series of the erection of Gothic cathedrals, the career of criminals, or lists of publications by scientists as well as catalogues of works by artists. The basic figure of Kondratiev's cycle appears everywhere, which models growth, maturity and decline in logistic curves. The 'internal clock' of the activity of social innovation which Marchetti thinks he has found indicates, towards the end of a period of recession, at the rock bottom of the sine curve, at the same time the beginning of the next wave of innovation. With its rise, new markets open up for the products it will produce, and it leads to the creation of new jobs and investments. This 'mega-breathing' of society can be explained – in so far as Marchetti enters into explanations – from the perspective of the theory of evolution: not just in the biological process of evolution, but also in the social one there are niches which are to be found at different levels of abstraction. Whether bacteria, cars or mega-technologies for the production of energy – the observed populations first grow into niches which they try to 'colonize'. In doing so, they are never completely alone – other rivals are either already in the niche or equally push their way in. A logistic equation, named after Lotka-Volterra, describes the relation between the size of the colonizing population and the speed of growth at which it approaches saturation point. It is essentially a question of processes of diffusion, since they are easier to measure and count than mutations (technological innovations) or selections (the testing of innovation). In case a niche is already full, the ensuing rival has good prospects of being able successfully to oust the less efficient population and ultimately to fill the niche.

It is that simple: everything follows the logistic curve, as Haldane had shown for biology as early as 1924. The successful rivals owe their growth to it, the losers their death.[26]

Undoubtedly, the study of these and similar phenomena of (predictable) recurrence – however one may judge its result or the methods used to attain it – holds a powerful intellectual fascination, one which thrilled even the early statisticians, then still wholly 'because of the beauty of God', which seemed discernible in birth rates and death rates (Süßmilch).[27] But there is more at stake than the fascination of scientific predictions, if one is to be able to take successful action in social life which is so inscrutable, or to be able to discover the beauty of regularities beyond the will or the intention of human beings.

The search for the 'internal clock', the proper time of technologies and whole techno-systems which arise, grow and perish by being superseded by subsequent, retrospectively superior ones, is the attempt to find the time discipline of cyclical recurrence and to use it by trying to acquire it. It is furthermore the attempt to get to grips with those problems which were denied by linearity: to explain breaks and discontinuities, compared with which the discovery of curves of growth and decline is relatively simple. To be on the trail of the proper time of a series of technological, scientific or artistic innovations, or of a whole 'system' of works, also means internalizing the time discipline contained in such regularities to the point where they can be included in what 'can be advanced by means of method, organization and institution, and condensed by means of acceleration', as it was formulated at the beginning of the machine age. Only it is no longer a question of acceleration alone. Deceleration can also be appropriate, depending on whether the product is in the phase of 'youth', 'maturity' or 'senescence'. The use of anthropomorphic terms like these in the relevant literature by economists[28] indicates how much the investigation of the 'life cycles' of technologies has become a self-evident part of marketing strategies and analyses. Striving for a 'prolonged product adolescence' can definitely be in the interests of the American economy in a particular phase of its competition with Japan; and not just in this, of course.

What a difference between the time discipline which was to the fore during the machine age and that which industrial production envisages today: during the industrial revolution, time discipline consisted in the mostly forced and painful habituation of people to the temporal requirements of the machine and its economic conditions of production. It presupposed the laborious learning of punctuality, to which children were habituated at school from an early age – as a preparation for working life – a process which was implemented with brutal methods and required an extremely long time to lead to that internalization which has become a matter of course today. Punctuality as a temporal 'virtue' no longer exists today; it is expected as an element of self-discipline from all members of society who want to take part in working life. Efforts are no longer concentrated on human beings today, but on the prerequisites for and consequences of the activity of innovation in terms of temporal organization. The timetable in the life cycle of a product or a market is to be investigated and then made controllable. The physical and mental adaptability of human beings is presupposed; they are already sufficiently disciplined with regard to time. What now has to follow is the adaptability of institutions: marketing, the influencing of tastes and of fashions, the programming of artificial obsolescence in a society which has already been familiarized with 'disposability'. Innovations and markets are to be subordinated to the temporal discipline of rise, saturation and decline; beforehand one has to learn it, and in order to be able to learn it, it has to be investigated.

The life cycles of technologies are confronted with other super-cycles and epicycles in the financial sphere, where risk capital has to be created and 'destroyed' in order to keep the profitable cycle alive. Viewed thus, the production of goods and services, of jobs and of capital, obeys a single cycle of enormous complexity, controlled by the individual life cycles of the subsystems, and decided at the 'right' moments of buying and selling. A remarkably complex institutionally controlled management of time attempts to recognize these cyclical interconnections in their temporal interdependences, in order then to be able to implement the strategy of the controlled interval. This is the attempt to achieve a planned and managed growth by controlling its speed, and in the knowledge that as a result of the built-in cyclicality growth will be followed by decline, and obsolescence. If it is possible to learn to control acceleration in a cycle, then time discipline becomes ever more extensible. Chronobiology and chronosociology are joined by chronotechnology. This has little use for the linearity of the machine age. What is interesting is no longer the individual worker in interaction with the machine when the so-called man-machine-system has long since been incorporated into a larger organizational complex, but the proper times through which phases of innovation occur in institutional and organizational time discipline. Biological metaphors should not tempt us to see linearity as 'hard' and cyclicality as 'soft' time discipline. As with the chronology of history, they bear no content, they are – to begin with – empty.

Modelling of processes by means of statistical methods, heuristics and simulation increasingly deals with the phenomenon of the unexpected, of discontinuous processes and of surprises. Linear extrapolations of trends, derived with the aid of parameters from a combination of temporal series and comparable sectoral analyses of the existing system, are regarded as inadequate for the portrayal of changes at the level of the world system – climatic and ecological, demographic or economic ones. Instead of prediction which can be derived in linear terms, the focus of interest is possible deviation and the regularity which might perhaps be found in it. Surprises can happen to individuals, institutions or whole societies. To be able to incorporate them in predictions increases the range of possible measures in order to be prepared for them. The cycle between prediction, even of the unexpected, and possible control begins to come full circle: it is the question of the extended present.

In the meantime, however, it is necessary to cope with the surprises which have already occurred. In retrospect, one of the biggest surprises is probably the realization that even progress can age. In Robert Jungk's pun, progress has become pro-dross. Incessant innovation creates new problems of obsolescence. Ageing and obsolete industries, the regions in which they are established and on which they have left their mark, like the increasingly ubiquitous rubbish dumps, are a conspicuous expression of the other side of innovation. Storing the most dangerous waste materials has become a detective game with lethal consequences in the oceans. If the predictions about the end of the current Kondratiev cycle are to be believed, around the year 1995 not only will a new phase of intensive technological innovation begin, but many firms will also 'die' as organizational units, and many jobs will be 'destroyed'. The social cost of these and other ageing processes is high. Just like the phenomenon of human and social ageing in view of an ageing population in the industrial nations, it is only slowly coming to public awareness. This results in a new social, and not just individual, experience. The level of expectations of a not inconsiderable minority is shrinking solely because of their advanced age, while the ageing process of technologies is being accelerated by succeeding technological innovations.

Ageing is measured on a socially accepted scale of reference, which is generally the chronological one of calendar time. But this level of abstraction is not very meaningful when it is a question of grasping the social and individual differences which come to light. Above all, the cultural definition intervenes which distinguishes ageing from 'becoming obsolete'. Becoming obsolete means ageing more quickly than is to be expected from the average rates of ageing or is prescribed by the norm. If technologies, firms and regions age more quickly and clearly 'become obsolete' today, just like people's professional qualifications and the knowledge acquired in their lifetime, then it seems reasonable to suppose that the norm of ageing changes according to the amount of innovation. The faster the rate of innovation, the faster the growth of proneness to obsolescence.

This gives rise to the problem of the cultural maturity of a society, among other things, which is shown by whether it learns to overcome its own problems of waste. The French palaeontologist Leroi-Gourhan gives an impressive description of an evolutionary leap in this respect from the early days of mankind. 'We possess', he writes,

> precise records of three dwelling places of the Moustérien, one of them situated in the open air in Moldovo on the Dnjestr, two in caves: in the Grotte de l'Hyène and in the Grotte du Renne of Arcy-sur-Cure in Yonne. They differ considerably in form: the dwelling place in the USSR is a circular area roughly eight metres in diameter, evidently the site of a tent or a hut; the dwelling place in the hyena cave lies in a hall five to six metres in diameter, and that of the reindeer cave lies in part of a gallery two metres wide and five to six metres long. Despite these differences, the three dwelling places show a striking conformity. They consist of a central area in which the fireplaces are situated and which is relatively free of animal remains, but full of stone tools; this central area is surrounded by a dense belt of scraped and smashed bones. If we disregard the structure which must have existed in Moldovo, then the reconstruction yields a very meagre picture. Neanderthal man lived surrounded by the remains of his hunting quarry, which he pushed away a bit in order to create a space to live in.

The contrast to the dwelling places from the period around 30,000 BC could not be greater:

> The whole space is carefully cleaned; outside, we come across some heaps of bigger rubbish and, scattered over the slopes, the 'rubbish dumps', little piles of ashes, interspersed with flakes of stone and tiny fragments of bone. The moment in evolution at which the first pictorial representations appear is thus simultaneously the point when the living space is marked off from the chaos of its surroundings. The role of the human being as an organizer of space appears here in its systematic arrangement.[29]

If we agree with Leroi-Gourhan that the organization of inhabited space is not a question of mere technological convenience but, in the same sense as language, the symbolic expression of universal human behaviour, then clearly the three requirements regarding the dwelling place were successfully met for the first time here: 'to create technologically efficient surroundings, . . . to give the social system a framework and . . . to create order in the surrounding universe from a single point'.[30] Can the solution to the problem of waste incurred in each case be regarded even today as one of the turning points of cultural evolution? Whole branches of industry are engaged in disposing of waste in modern industrial civilization, transporting it away, re-storing it and permanently disposing of it. Science and technology offer new methods of cyclically built-in waste utilization, where in a closed system the waste incurred – no matter whether gaseous, liquid, or in solid form – is to be transformed in such a way that it is either used again in production, or reaches the outside world only in safe remnants. A particular problem is the waste whose toxicity persists over long periods of time, and which loses its endangering potential only very slowly. Will the process of civilization, described by Norbert Elias as the gradual transformation of outside constraints into self-constraints, which took place in the course of the increasing integration of human interactions and the setting up of monopolies on the part of the central powers who were establishing themselves, be continued in the extension of individual standards of cleanliness beyond the territorial confinement to the domestic sphere controllable by oneself? The historical process of civilization is an example of a blind but directed, long-term social process which runs otherwise than intended, and whose ultimate results were neither foreseeable nor intended in this form by those involved.

Today, from the varied point of view of those involved which results not least from very different fields of interest, it seems clear what is desirable. But equally the obstacles in the path of any overall plan, however well intended, and any 'grand design', are insurmountable. The effects of waste production know neither spatially territorial nor temporal limits, they ignore the sovereign rights of nation-states and the time spans of parliamentary terms. But the control mechanisms which can emanate from state authorities via statutory regulations like laws or prohibitions, or can be steered via the market through economic incentives, are either territorially restricted or, as in the case of multinational companies, hard to bring under a particular state jurisdiction. Households and individuals can, for their part, admittedly change their social awareness and feel responsible for further domains of action than the one which is directly their own, but action and awareness bear a peculiar relation to one another, determined by further circumstances: insight into the problem alone does not suffice to entail appropriate action. Scientific and technological solutions, on the other hand, which are among the most important vehicles of evolution, do not for their part occur in a social vacuum. Market conditions and economic interests, lead times for development and competitive relations with already existing waste technologies characterize the multiple interdependences between economics, science and technology. The transformation of outside constraints into internalized, yet also individualized self-constraints is probably not sufficient to bring about an advance in civilization in the face of the problem of waste. Collectively anchored self-constraints, on the other hand, require the invention of new institutions and institutional mechanisms of coordination and control. They can neither be constructed voluntarily, nor do they occur in an antisocial sphere. They arise as a social process taking account of existing power structures, which are reproduced and yet continue to become differentiated, under certain conditions.

One of these, the temporal condition, is the increase in the urgency of the problem in conjunction with the cyclicality imputed to innovative events. The regular production of waste is foreseeable. The postulate holds good here, too, of 'being able to comprehend' the prerequisite for the 'uniqueness of one's own surprise', in order to be prepared for it. In an age obsessed with innovation, the ageing of products, technologies and abilities, the formation of waste, is no surprise any more. But what follows this comprehension? One solution consists in the attempt to control the ageing process in temporal terms. 'Successful ageing' is the appropriate motto coined for the human ageing process. Through an artificial acceleration or deceleration of particular functions and processes, negative effects can be outweighed; through knowledge of the different proper times of systems or sub-systems, better temporal coordinations can be achieved. But the underlying problem, which was long concealed by the linearity of the machine age, is of a more general nature. In comparison with organisms or organic components, the machine could feign indefatigability and immortality. In a different sphere of production, the symbolic one, this could never happen in the same way. Artistic production has never gone along with the linearity of the machine. Works of art, or rather their elements, can be arranged in the form of sequences, as art historian George Kubler suggests in an interesting analysis, which represent in their turn stylistic directions which supersede one another. Every stylistic direction, every sequence, from the revolutionary new beginning, via mature development to final decay, is composed of connected phenomena which represent the attempt to find answers and provide solutions to quite specific problems of form or content. Cyclical succession is highly sophisticated, since for every sequence which determines a stylistic direction it is also necessary to find an answer to the following problem:

> The occurrence of things is governed by our changing attitudes towards the processes of invention, repetition and discard. Without invention there would only be stale routine. Without copying there would never be enough of any man-made thing, and without waste or discard too many things would outlast their usefulness. Our attitudes towards these processes are themselves in constant change, so that we confront the double difficulty of charting changes in things, together with tracing the change in ideas about change.[31]

Kubler's analysis is aimed at aesthetics and not the 'useful inventions', as he calls them, of technology. But there are definitely similarities, mediated by 'our attitude' towards these processes. The inherent tension between repetition, the desire to return to familiar patterns, and invention as the desire to escape from habit through new variations, characterizes symbolic production no less than the technological kind. It is the basis of the complementarity between linearity and cyclicality. The individual is protected by society against too many variations by a complex and subtle structure of routine and habits. But many examples can all too easily be cited, beginning with the *tourbillon social* of the industrial revolution, in which this tension gets out of balance and turns into extremes. And what about the decision to throw things away, to eliminate them from circulation? Throwing away always also comprises a change of values, since something that was once valuable is thereby degraded. Earlier societies partly developed elaborate rituals in order to preserve things. The burial objects and funeral cults of many cultures in prehistoric times bear witness to this. Today many things are thrown away, of course, but others are under preservation orders: objects of daily use, animals and knowledge suddenly acquire the value of antiques because they belong to a culture which is in the process of disappearing. At the end of a cycle there is thus not necessarily a void: there are symbolic and real possibilities of storing in the collective memory at least a part of the 'population' threatened with destruction, or giving it a place in the museums, like the burial objects which were supposed to accompany the dead on their way in the other world.

The fascinating recurrence of the cyclical, and the investigations which aim systematically to bring to light the 'internal clock' in the succession of technological artefacts, of ideas or of art objects, and to specify the proper time of populations and systems – all of these do not exempt a society from facing up to the question of the orchestration of these cycles. On the contrary. The problem of waste makes it all too obvious that in every society the relative speeds at which innovation, repetition and obliteration, i.e. destruction, occur have to be counterbalanced against one another. It is not just a question of making relative weightings. With the abolition of the category of the open future, which predominated in the machine age under the notion of the linearity of time, all three processes crowd into the extended present. The denser the rate of innovation in the present, the more waste in the material and metaphorical sense is to be expected, and the more problems with waste disposal will have to be solved – likewise in the present. With the rediscovery of the cyclical and the extension of the present, attempts at a social solution have been set in motion to produce mechanisms in time for a new balance between the processes of invention, repetition and throwing away. Inventions, that is technological

innovations, are desirable precisely in their unpredict-
ability, but their positive and negative repercussions have
to be recognized and controlled as early as possible. In
temporal terms, the capacity for prognostication of this
early recognition is compressed into a period of technological genesis in which the possibilities already reveal
themselves, but can still be worked on and shaped: the
time of becoming in the extended present. The problems
of waste press for early recognition and prevention, for
pre-emption before waste becomes such. But can waste be
recognized and disposed of right at the beginning of a
curve of innovation? Innovation has to be translated from
uncontrolled technological and social growth into planned
and rationalized reform. The problem of waste is even
harder to handle if it has to be solved at the very beginning
of the process of innovation by techniques of avoidance or
disposal. From a certain order of magnitude on, the cost of
waste disposal can no longer be externalized. More order
and control, more management of processes, are on
the agenda here too, where everything presses for early
recognition, prevention and pre-emption. But what selec-
tivity is required here, and who determines the criteria to
be employed? And who will guarantee that with the weeds
inherent in the uncontrolled growth the roots of creativity
are not removed as well?

In the machine age, the notion of the linearity of time
prevailed because time, following the laws of economics,
was equated with money for the first time and thus made
into a scarce resource. Time = money was at work in the
motions of the machines, and these produced incessantly
towards an open horizon of the future. In the nineteenth
century, science, technology and industry had become
an empirically redeemable substratum for the idea of
progress. The general empirical theorem of scientific and
technological inventions was that they promised further
progress without being able to calculate it exactly in advance. Indeed, it was precisely the fact that future progress

could not be experienced which was empirically verified, as it were; its calculable unknownness secured the conclusiveness of its actual occurrence.[32]

Today, however, the urgent desire prevails to recognize the consequent effects as early as possible even in the extended present, in order to steer them into desired or undesired channels. So much that is new has been and is being produced that the old is becoming too much. Hence the pressure for limitation is growing. Finiteness is entering into the conceptions of time. But it is not enough, following linear thinking, to remain confined to quantities or to labour under the illusion that the answer is to produce less. Cyclicality seeks to provide a remedy here. It offers a point of view in which the necessity is taken into account, theoretically at least, of making the processes of innovation predictable as early as possible, in order to learn to control the prerequisites for one's own surprises. The present is thereby extended further. But transforming the moment of becoming into the decisive point of selection holds dangers which result from the inadequacy of the instruments of diagnosis and prognosis, and from the multiplicity, still good for surprises, which results from the possibility of human behaviour. Creativity has many forms of expression, errors must remain tolerable and systems amenable to error. The other option attempts to come to terms with the end, to risk the evolutionary leap, and to find solutions for the problem of waste and obsolescence which are suited to a scientific and technological culture. Here, too, the quantitatively linear point of view is not sufficient which seeks merely to preserve, for how much and what can be crammed into museums, classified as a historical monument, artificially stored in reserves? Hence it is a question of the conversion of energy, matter and knowledge. It is a question of the revaluation and transformation of waste, of technological procedures for this as well as institutional economic incentives and a changed social awareness. The cyclical conception of time offers the model of flowing back into the cyclical process, of recycling. Time is so construed here that it is the finiteness of a variety of cycles, which mutually influence one another in their features and can be influenced by human behaviour. At the end, after decay or completion, something new can begin. But the new is no longer as light-heartedly new as the belief in progress once promised. It is new material into which old material flows, not as a past continuing to have a linear effect, as the lead weight of a tradition, but as recycled proper time of a cycle of innovation. Only thus can new social forms of existence emerge from the proliferation of multiple times: in the extended present instead of in the future.

3

Cronos's Fear of the New Age

Every finite knowledge . . . encounters the same boundary in the
case of dynamically chaotic systems: after a period of evolution,
which results from the intrinsic dynamics of the system, the
concept of individual development loses its meaning; what remains is solely the statistical calculation of the probabilities of
evolution.
  Ilya Prigogine and Isabelle Stengers, *Entre le Temps et l'Eternité*

When the sociologists of science were preparing to go into
the laboratories in order to observe scientists at work
directly on the spot, other questions were to the fore than
those under discussion here. Like anthropologists who
seek out an unknown tribe to get themselves initiated into
its mysterious customs, in order thus to learn to understand exotic symbolic constructs, they first wanted to
check the meaning of the conventional distinction between 'scientific' knowledge and the 'non-scientific' kind.
Even if the great 'epistemological break' in Gaston
Bachelard's sense, which distinguishes the savage thought
of humanity from that distorted by science and separates
amateurs from experts, was not totally to be denied, it was
at least to be relativized. What, apart from the door to the
laboratory, separates the world of science from society?
It was undeniable that the muttering of incantations by
the local sorcerer on the Ivory Coast, or his meticulous
inspection of a dead person, differed in their effect from
the treatment of a cancer patient with laser therapy or the
investigation of a gene with the aid of a DNA probe in a
Californian laboratory. The sciences operate with a far
greater degree of efficiency than the sum total of everything which the practice of magic and socio-religious

empathy ever had to offer before. But what is the cause of this enormous difference in effect? What was so enticing about the laboratory was to trace the inroads made by society into this sphere. Through the investigation of social practices, of the social influence on the generative process of knowledge, one intended to gain insights in order better to understand how science attains its effectiveness and how 'natural reality', which does not belong to the social order, is nevertheless constituted by the social generative process.

In the course of these observational inquiries and expeditions of discovery into the territory of the laboratory, previously entered only by scientific 'natives' and which is devoted to the generation of scientific knowledge, what presented itself to observation was pre-eminently that which was visible: the activities of the scientists, their technical practice in handling apparatus, in measuring and checking natural processes which – invisible to begin with – are made visible only by the processes of measurement. The sociologists of science further encountered what was entered and written down. Notes and diagrams of all kinds, photographs and pictures which are produced with the aid of information technologies.

These notes give insights both into the deep structure and into the surface composition of the phenomena investigated: they reproduce what had been 'entered' by means of the process of measurement into the apparatus constructed for this purpose. But the 'signs' thus registered have to be read and interpreted. The discussion between scientists serves this purpose, their 'negotiation' conducted together, which finally leads to a process of 'manufacture of facts': through the transcription of what has been ascertained and mediated so far, the scientific text emerges which, with the publication aspired to in a scientific journal, is turned at last into what, though discussible and criticizable, is still a 'fact'.[1]

Such a schematic course of the process of scientific work in the laboratory, as observed and interpreted by sociologists of science, is based on a spatial model which has also been explicitly elaborated by Bruno Latour, one of the most famous spokesmen of this approach.[2] According to him, the success of the natural sciences, in comparison with other methods of creating knowledge, is based on the fact that they manage to make a portion of natural phenomena 'mobile', to extract them from the natural locality where they are found, and to transport them to the laboratory. What science creates in this process is mobile, transportable nature. Sometimes things and phenomena change their form, their substance or other properties during this process. Distortions can arise which ought to be corrected again if possible. For what is desired is indeed mobile nature, which nevertheless is to be preserved unchanged in its nature. Nature made mobile is to be brought into the laboratory as invariantly as possible. For only there are its motions committed to paper. The answers given by nature to the experimental conditions can be recorded as traces or images. Photographs fix series of movements, and much that is large in nature can be reduced in the laboratory to the scale of human perception: by means of the central process of miniaturization, it is increasingly possible to fetch more phenomena into the laboratory. This development signals a general trend according to which all the sciences are developing into 'laboratory science': with the aid of computer-based imaging technologies or space telescopes, they are even able, as in the case of astronomy, to become independent of observation in the field to a certain extent.[3]

There are two working measures which, in the opinion of sociologists of science, cause the success of the natural sciences: on the one hand, along these lines more and more of nature made mobile is being brought into the laboratory, and on the other, accompanying this, there is a growing ability to increase the information value which nature provides under laboratory conditions by means of appropriate questions and processing methods. What is 'spatial' about this process is first the transport and the transfer of a portion of nature to the laboratory. Just as the explorers used to return with their captured specimens or at least with drawings and detailed descriptions of the wonderful things they had seen during their investigations, so today nature is brought into the laboratory with the aid of remote-controlled viewing and collecting instruments. The acceleration potential inherent in this process essentially results from the organization of work: transportation occurs more and more, and more and more quickly. But there is also a temporal dimension to this process. The capacity for acceleration of the process of generating knowledge also stems from the fact that the natural phenomena gathered in form a cultural relation with the researchers, and that they receive a share of their temporality, of the social time of the laboratory. Through the illustration and digitalization which accompany their transportation, the objects of investigation are brought into the procedural context of the laboratory, where they are kept continuously present:

> The integration and new constitution of objects of investigation in the interactional environment of the laboratory is, incidentally, connected with an increase in the possibilities of articulation. Interactional environments are temporally structured environments capable of acceleration, which are specified by the sequence of the changes in articulation of the participants.[4]

Because today, scattered over the whole world, researchers are linked up with observational and measurement data which are obtained from space, for instance by means of electronic transmission, then circulated and exchanged, it becomes possible to work simultaneously on a common 'knowledge front'.

It is an open question whether this extreme form of simultaneity built into the division of labour is a peculiarity of astronomy, for even Kepler offered Fabricius the use of his observational data in 1608 with the laconic question 'what if we cannot all do everything?'[5] The built-in mechanism of competition also undoubtedly contributes to the acceleration of the generation of knowledge. But the really remarkable thing which results from the observations of the scientific laboratory is not so much the integration of the objects of investigation brought to the laboratory into the social temporality of the researchers, and into a work organization which strives for a division of labour with an approximative simultaneity, for in this respect the scientific research process resembles other industrial methods of production. The remarkable thing is rather not just that a separate space has arisen in the laboratory, linked by means of miniaturization and other techniques with distant, larger or smaller spaces in nature, but that a separate time-structure is created in the laboratory. Because it is possible to keep the objects of investigation continuously present in the procedural context of the laboratory, the temporal conditions of experimentation and possibilities of control over them are considerably extended. If the time-structures of an object become manipulable by experiment, its capacity for articulation increases. In the artificially producible present, other time-scales become observable, sequences repeatable, processes possible to accelerate or slow down. In the laboratory, science creates its own time, which is not to be equated with the 'cultural forms of interaction' or the 'local temporality' of the researchers themselves. The laboratory time created for the investigation and interpretation of phenomena rather itself becomes a scientific and cultural construct, which begins to react upon the temporality of society at the latest when the objects of investigation, in however changed a form, leave the laboratory and continue to have an effect as artefacts in society. Laboratory time then brings its own need for time with it. This is directed, as in the laboratory itself, towards constant availability, accessibility and continuous presence.

This has not always been the case. The sciences, as
Blumenberg notes, announced their need for time very
early on, indeed this partly even stands for the transition to
modern science. But at first it was a need for time and a
time-structure which was directed towards the past, which
was intended to catch up on what reason thought it
needed at the time of the Enlightenment. It was never a
question here of procuring and creating time for the sake
of pure knowledge alone. If the sciences have known how
to meet their need for time successfully, then it is always
because the time-structures discovered and created by
them, and their peculiarities, had retroactive effect and
were anchored in socio-economic connections, and in a
practice through which every need for time on the part of
science that was met became translatable into a societal
need and demand for these very time-structures. They
range from the rampant ideology of the machine age to
concrete working-time regulations invoking it; from the
logic of the pair of compasses, in which time is a succession of moments, and the actual change occurs when
the eyes are shut, to the high-speed calculator. In historical
terms, astronomy, which had tried as early as Kepler and
Copernicus to reconcile the empirical observational data
with the requirements of theory but also with a coming
social 'turning point', was followed by geology. Today, it
is the broad front of knowledge of the laboratory sciences
which, increasingly interlocked with society and economics, anticipatingly articulates, moulds and puts into
operation its need for time – as laboratory time. In the
1830s, there was a heated scientific controversy which
began with a seemingly minor problem in the dating of
geological strata in the English county of Devon, and
ended with a new perspective on the history of the earth.[6]
But in order to comprehend the extent of the change in the
understanding of the past with real, economic consequences for the present at that time, it must be recalled
that the creation of the geological time-scale took place in

a remarkably brief and dense period of scientific work in less than half a century. Around 1800, science admittedly knew that the earth was old, but there was no frame of reference at all to arrange historical events in their chronological sequence. The determining criterion generally accepted since then, based on the chronological order of fossils, did not yet exist. It was as if historians knew that there had been earlier civilizations on this earth, but had no idea whether the pyramid of Cheops had been erected before the cathedral of Chartres or not. Around 1850, however, history was a well-ordered sequence, embracing the whole world, of unrepeatable and recognizable events. It was defined by the history of life on earth, and established by a fixed nomenclature which was valid from New York to Moscow.[7]

The truly remarkable thing about this period of the 'discovery of time' through geology, however, was that the past was scientifically safeguarded precisely at a moment when one of the greatest social experiments in Europe began: the phase of intensive industrialization and its side effects, whereby the social present and future of millions of people was swept into the swirling current of commencing modernization and profoundly shaken.

In view of this coincidence, it also becomes less astonishing that the conflicts between geology and established religion over a literal interpretation of the story of the Creation were limited. Of course, there was a small minority which insisted on it, but it stood no chance in the face of a pragmatic science for which even a concept like 'creation' caused no difficulties, even if it could not be precisely translated into scientific terms. 'Creation' was to prove problematic only where, as in the case of Lamarck, no creative activity was allowed to exist any longer behind the natural process of evolution, before fully flaring up in the controversy surrounding Darwin's theory of evolution. The harmlessness and casualness with which geology asserted its conception of time in the face of religion in the first half of the nineteenth century did not hold good, however, for other relations of this science to the society of its time. The establishing and ordering of the strata of the earth had highly practical economic significance, for it formed the prerequisite for the discovery and extraction of raw materials which were imperative for incipient industrialization. One of the protagonists of the 'Great Devonian Controversy', Murchison, was adviser to the tsar of Russia, for example, and convinced him of the futility of looking for coal in a Silurian rock stratum.

Geology discovered time as the natural history of the earth, but only through the activity of scientists could this discovery be translated into practice. The historical connection which existed between the scientific concern with the 'natural time' of the earth on the one hand, and the industrial revolution on the other, went deeper, however, than the finding of coal leads us to assume. For Geoffrey Bowker, at any rate, who has conducted a semiotic investigation into the temporal perceptions of English and French geologists in the 1830s, it is obvious that the time discovered by the geologists soon turned into an ideological justification of the new conception of time which had infiltrated society.

The discourse which took place within geology about the beginnings of time turned it into a key science in the legitimation of the new social system of time which entered society with machines. Bowker reconstructs a fascinating picture from contemporary scientific texts by geologists on both sides of the English Channel. He shows how through a series of analogies and linguistic transformations God, the Creator in his relationship with his creation, was gradually replaced by a different analogous relationship, that which is established between the scientist and his creation, the machine. Science appropriates the beginning of natural time so to speak, by placing itself at the beginning instead of religion. It has to define this beginning afresh and thereby becomes the creator.[8]

Time becomes time which has flowed, slowly been petrified, entered into sediments and deposits, and it fixes a beginning which can be dated for the history of the earth and of human beings. There thus arises at the same time the linear continuum, to which all other series of movements refer. But the decisive step is taken by the analogy with the machine. It becomes the vehicle of natural time when the series of movements prescribed by physics are built into it. It thereby becomes the regulator of the social time system of human beings, who have to conform to it. The time-structure of the linear, homogenized, arbitrarily divisible continuum is transferred through the machine from the realm of nature to that of society. The scientist feeds into the machine, which is his creation, the time of nature, whereby it was endowed with a temporal ordering power in the face of which all other social notions of time would prove inferior, if not impotent. In the social chaos which resulted from the industrial revolution and which was to lead society to the edge of the collapse of its old structures, science and technology became that authority and ordering power which appeared to be the saviour from collapse. In its name and in that of progress, there has been a demand ever since for the submission to a system of time which invoked natural time, and in accordance with which both machines and human beings had to move. The machine age, with its dominant conception of linear time, was able to remain unchallenged for so long not least because of this 'successful' connection between natural and social time, established by the transformation of the scientific conception of time.

The ousting of religion as a time-setting authority, and as the highest authority in determining time, thus had far-reaching consequences. Nobody would question the monopoly of definition on the part of science today, which since 1967, for example, has given the definition of a second as 9,192,631,770 periods of the caesium atom. Even if there are still various strange-seeming rearguard actions by religious fundamentalists, as in the USA, which find expression in so-called 'creationism', attempts at a regressive departure from the scientific conception of time have no chance, and no significant consequences.

In historical terms, the establishment of the scientific conception of time, which for its part bears the stamp of a particular epoch of the history of science and of the social forces of its time, and its incorporation into what became the dominant social conception of time, had succeeded. Once the linear system of time was set in the form of a chronology going back to the newly fixed beginnings, acceleration could start in the form of motion making everything dynamic, which seemed to stop at nothing. In the *tourbillon social* which broke out with the industrial revolution and wrenched people out of their countless 'small worlds', out of the small towns and villages with self-contained social structures and forms of existence, and kindled in them the insatiable desire for growth, when everything, as Marx wrote, 'was pregnant with its own contradiction', acceleration became the experience of modernization overshadowing and shaping everything else. The pace becomes more important than the destination: anyone who stands firm stands still; everything, above all time, becomes frantic motion: the new myth was speed.

In view of this wildly spreading acceleration, it is not surprising that many people reacted to it with a kind of culture 'shock', and the phenomenon of 'shock' itself was derived from the medical diagnosis of the physical and mental state of victims injured in railway accidents.[9] But our subject here is not to be the collisions of the psyche and of countless existences with the locomotive of time, nor the countless metaphors with which people sought to put into words what they experienced as a gigantic torrent of motion, but the iconography of time. Artists have left behind images which are capable of expressing feelings more clearly than words.

These are pictures in which dying time is portrayed, truth as the daughter of time as well as time devouring its children. They are marked by irony and melancholy, but artists are also required to interpret them for us today and allow us to read them afresh. In his poetic and philosophical essay, Massimo Cacciari refers to a portrait of dying time from 1764 by the English satirist William Hogarth, and to two pictures by Goya which were produced as part of the Quinta del Sordo cycle. For Cacciari, time, portrayed as Cronos, reveals in its progress the truth of its own death. In Hogarth's picture, there is even the will, which bequeathes 'all and every Atom' not to God (these words are deleted) but to 'Chaos whom I appoint my sole Executor'. Beside the emaciated Cronos there lie the pipe which has slipped from his grasp and the blunt scythe; the hour-glass has run out; the world is already in ruins. Cupid's bow is smashed to pieces, and the bell has cracked. The world is going up in smoke. Time has condemned itself to the *'consummatus est'*; in the end it feels itself to be void. In Goya's pictures, according to Cacciari, what is portrayed is the folly of time. Large black eyes stare at the void which is now looming. In order to be able to survive, time is voracious, and in its insatiable greed it no longer even spares its own children. In order to survive, it also destroys the sole guarantee of its continuance. The same principle which justifies its existence condemns it to death. Time which consumes and destroys, in order to be able to live, is characterized by 'folly': it crazily rushes to its own destruction. Its death wish manifests itself in a desperate and blind will to live. Cacciari exhorts the beholders of Goya's figure to 'liberating laughter', to laughter which reveals the folly of time and thereby exposes its self-destructive mechanism: 'Voracious time reveals the untruth of human claims to immortal and unchangeable values. The moment of that laughter which begins to liberate us is only attainable if we comprehend the anti-idolatrous truth which portrays destroying time.'[10]

But why does time die of its own mortality? What makes it aware of the latter? Also in the first portrayal Cacciari chooses, in Hogarth's picture, time is dying. With the last breath from the mouth of Cronos, while all around in the midst of a ruin everything lies devastated, the values of the world prove to be mortal products of time. But what has caused this self-destruction?

Like all artistic masterpieces, these too remain open, despite poetic and philosophical interpretations, to readings and further questions, even to those which come from other systems of discourse. A Cronos who wants to survive commits the unpardonable folly of consuming his own stock, his own children. Shock sits in his wide-open eyes, in his emaciated body. And what was the great thunderbolt which not only carries off Hogarth's hoary Cronos but has laid the whole world, *finis mundi*, in ruins, legally sealed before being handed over to chaos? If all existing values are destroyed in the process, as Hogarth depicts with delicate irony, if all hopes of continued existence are vain, what has caused this collapse? What does the iconography of the new age look like, the semantics of which does not yet enter the picture, but whose temporalized movement is already perceptible as a concept of history? In another painting by Goya, triumphant truth – is it the daughter of Cronos? – is depicted as a young, naked female figure. Cronos is still holding her by the hand, but he himself, furnished with large wings, has to give way. In the foreground sits history as a witness narrating the events, but what radiant young truth is it which Cronos has to release from his clutches?

The new age, which is mentioned increasingly more often from the second half of the eighteenth century, manifests itself through a new concept of time and becomes the distinctive feature of an epoch which succinctly describes itself as the 'modern age': 'Time does not just remain the form in which all stories take place, it gains a historical quality itself. History then no longer takes place in time, but through time. Time is dynamized into a force of history itself.'[11] It is recognized and accepted by contemporaries as the modern age. It manifests itself by being able to produce something new, and this is first of all – new knowledge. The old structure of knowledge, which extended from the early Middle Ages into the nineteenth century, was based on the principle of preserving the stock, of incorporation and storage in the great encyclopaedic and classificatory tradition. For Voltaire, the Encyclopaedia was still an 'everlasting' and unsurpassable 'inventory of human capacities'. In 1767, when the enterprise was still by no means finished, Voltaire stated that it was not just the first, but perhaps also the last example of its kind on earth. He saw it as containing the prerequisites, as regards theoretical content, for the final success of reason – the climax of human history, which admittedly still needed disseminating and implementing as a kind of post-history of uncertain duration.[12]

The new knowledge arises under changed conditions of creation and in changed structures of organization. It becomes disputable knowledge which has to lay itself open to criticism, and is capable of improvement through criticism. What is important is no longer how and at what point it can be incorporated in the existing ordered structure of total knowledge. It does not become true through true safe-keeping, but when it can be exposed to open argument and increasingly to the experimentally empirical test procedure by means of measurement and pieces of equipment, and can hold its own there. In accordance with its epistemological condition, it is a knowledge on call, and it bears within it the willingness to give up the position it has achieved at any time in favour of later, but better knowledge. It is a knowledge committed to scientific progress. The beginnings of the changed conditions for generating it lie in the eighteenth century, that period in which the decisive preconditions are created for the subsequent, dramatically increasing growth of scientific knowledge in particular, due to the systematic opening up of new sources of cognition and their methodical utilization. It is also a century, however, which is pervaded with a vast destruction of knowledge. Knowledge previously preserved only with great effort and protected by the aura of tradition increasingly comes under the pressure of experimental test conditions which it cannot withstand. In the eighteenth century, it first becomes apparent how the novelty of cognition begins to transform the standpoints of preservation and of previously valid classification. The newly tapped sources of cognition, the journeys and expeditions undertaken in the course of progressive colonialization, create curiosity about the new and lead almost inevitably to a change in the processing capacity of science. The old schemes of classification, based on generalization and classificatory abstraction, are no longer sufficient to absorb the partly exotic knowledge dragged in from all over the world, without bursting the conventional categories of classification. It is the century in which not just the 'birth of the clinic' takes place, but also that of the laboratory, that organizational invention for the purpose of generating knowledge, which gradually, confirmed by its successes, turns all science into laboratory science.

Henceforth, nature is not just observed, but reproduced and generated in the laboratory. With the revelation of what is invisible to begin with, the social construction of the natural world begins. A still substantially artificial 'auto-production of phenomena' commences, as Stichweh calls it, which not only prevails in the contest to oust the old, more rigid knowledge, but forms the basis of the scientific conception of the world which has been current since then.[13]

Was it perhaps this vision which so frightened Cronos that he turned to the last resort and staged his suicide by devouring his children, while the new age began its triumphal march and has been incessantly disgorging its children since then? Did the world of the old skinflint Cronos, as Hogarth portrays him with bitterly ironic mockery, sink in emotionally sublime fashion into the final state of proclaimed chaos because neither the accumulated property nor the values and virtues sustaining it were still assured of their continued existence, in the face of a new age which did not just practise accumulation for the sake of hoarding, but which was preparing to invest in order to turn all tied-up funds into liquid assets? The modern age and its characteristic form of motion, acceleration, did not content itself with frightening old Cronos by producing new knowledge, but it set to work in extremely pragmatic fashion to translate it into action. What Francis Bacon had already outlined with his patterns of argumentation – the hope for a systematic improvement of the sciences, if one strives to recognize not just the benefit for tomorrow but the causes forever, if one replaces chance with planning and then guides it towards a well-controlled progress of inventions, while providing mutual help through the division of labour – all this now began to be realized. The sciences became the key sector in which 'progress' or 'progression' could be continually registered during the following period.[14] Scientists and technologists began, as Bowker had said of geologists, to implement the new age, by incorporating faster and coordinated series of motions into machines. Acceleration was first of all that increase in motion which emanated from the machine and which immediately embraced all other areas of life, and thus became the empirically indisputable basis for the belief in progress.

What the Enlightenment lacked, a dynamic concept of economics, was now made good in economic practice. The period of transformation, which separates knowledge and research from application and use, became the driving element in capitalist competition geared to innovations, through the instrument of the market and with the aid of new contemporaries, the capitalist entrepreneurs. The entrepreneurs had devoted themselves to implementing whatever was new on the market at any one time and dedicated their work, in Joseph Schumpeter's succinctly coined phrase, to creative destruction. The entrepreneurs were shaped by the new age and its temporality. The element of creative destruction refers to the process of innovation itself, to the accelerated process of making way for new products and procedures. But what sustains the market in temporal terms, what constitutes its specific temporality, is the temporary cost advantage which the capitalist entrepreneur can expect. The motive force is profit. In Schumpeter's version, the entrepreneur knows how to gain a cost advantage – admittedly only a temporary one – with the aid of innovation in the face of the large number of traditionally oriented 'hosts of the economic cycle', who remain attached to the old, static order of the circulation of goods.[15] Entrepreneurial profit thus arises from the discrepancy between the market price prevailing on static markets and the individual cost price at which the entrepreneur can produce by virtue of innovation. Schumpeter wishes to trace the law of societal development, and he thinks that this law is indigenous to the sphere of economics. The final cause, and the motor of development, is the sporadically occurring changes, brought about by creative individuals, in the 'productive combination' of new goods, new methods of production, new markets and sources of raw materials, as well as the creation of new forms of organization, particularly those of monopolies. These new combinations lead sooner or later to institutional adaptations, which result in qualitative changes in the structure of society. Through entrepreneurial capitalism, according to this classical interpretation, business life is removed from a stationary state into one of perpetual dynamism, of continual innovation. As Schumpeter and other observers noticed, the innovations usually occur 'in droves': this results in the economic waves which had struck Marx and Kondratiev and others as a characteristic of economic development under capitalist circumstances. The abrupt changes in a previously stationary state lead to signs of an upswing in the economy which are only superseded by a counter-movement after some time. The 'occurrence in droves' of innovations, their bundling up in phases of innovation, is put down to the fact that countless imitators stick to the heels of the successful entrepreneur, and that the willingness of consumers to accept innovations grows in the course of time.

The analysis of innovatory activity has remained a hotly disputed subject. The heroic figure of the individual entrepreneur, who was the *deus ex machina* for Schumpeter, has given way to a more sophisticated viewpoint of complex, increasingly intertwined events, in which a technology based on scientific findings (science-based technology) and a mechanized science on the one hand, and the market on the other, operate in mutually reinforcing interaction. Even though individual technological or scientific 'breakthroughs' can be repeatedly identified, it has long since become clear that appropriate institutional, research-organizational and economic and financial prerequisites are needed in order to be able to hasten benefits from the point of view of the market. Instead of individual invention and its career, it is the dynamics of innovatory development, represented in the temporal trajectories of entire systems of technology, with the probabilities of their implementation, which shape the phenomenon of 'innovation' in terms both of science and technology and of social organization.[16]

The temporal peculiarity of innovations is still the fact that they are embedded in the competitive time of the market. Innovations which reach the market have entered the competitive field of economic forces from that moment on, and it is obvious how this force field increasingly is shifting into the offshore area of innovation-creating

research. From a macroscopic viewpoint, the contest to
ost one another then begins, the struggle for the niches,
whether of already existing and occupied markets or of
those still to be created, which are intended to react to
needs freshly to be aroused. Considered from a closer
viewpoint, it turns out that Schumpeter's distinction
between entrepreneurs as innovators and their 'mere imitators' has become completely blurred. Particularly in
high-tech fields, the buyers of technological innovations
are themselves highly discriminating customers, who for
their part can have a lasting influence on the innovative
product through their specific demand. But they are also
subject, as ultimately are all consumers – to the pressure of
competition. Acquiring a consumer item which has just
come on the market at a point in time before others do has
become a sign of distinction in the context of mass consumption, where the period of time that has elapsed in the
acquisition of goods determines the status of consumers.[17]
The small temporal difference expresses social distinctions, while big economic competition finds expression in
the international temporal advantage in the business of
scientific and technological innovation.

Acceleration in and through the machine, benefits
and profit through innovative temporal advantages in the
market, and temporal availability through the dissemination of 'laboratory time' in everyday life by means of
technological objects and artefacts, have become the
characteristic features of the dynamics of innovation. For
more and more of the work of scientific discovery which
takes place in the laboratory leaves its mark on the
technological objects and processes which then come on
to the market and enter the area of industrial production
and the everyday environment. More and more technological objects have something of 'laboratory time' about
them. It is characterized by the continuous presence of
objects and their constant temporal availability. They are
at hand round the clock and their temporal processes can
be checked, programmed, and articulated almost at will.

Under laboratory conditions, it is possible to accelerate things and slow them down; unique temporal events are possible as well as varied repetitions. Gradually, such temporal processes are also being introduced into society. Laboratory time is leaving its mark on the 'normal world'. Technological artefacts offer availability, but also demand availability of the human beings who operate them or at whose disposal they are supposed to be. The process of interdependence between machines and human beings is beginning to build up again.

In comparison with the living labour of animals or of human beings, every machine offers temporal availability which far exceeds that of the organic sphere. Technologies and technological artefacts are created by human beings and geared to particular ends. As a prerequisite and consequence of their being socially embedded, particular forms of organization of work are necessary or result from this, as well as particular knowledge, abilities, attitudes and behaviour in human beings who work on them or use them in everyday life. There is, as the sociology of industry and technology well knows, broad scope for the social shaping of technologies. These can be culturally determined, or can be shaped in economic and political terms. Of the built-in 'social constructions', of aims and normative ideas, habits and requirements which leave their mark on artefacts and which, particularly in feedback with the social organization in which they are used, reveal a complex behaviour pattern, the built-in dimension of time is surely one of the most fundamental dimensions. Technological artefacts are standardized, but they also standardize human and social behaviour. This standardization has long since included the area of private life beyond the workplace, and the distance which is to be covered between these two poles of individual and collective existence in industrialized countries.

At the same time, an almost symbiotic, complementary relationship is to be observed between social discipline, the rules and norms needed for maintaining it, and the standardizations which are already built into technologies. Here, too, the long-term societal development increasingly passes from a regulation which to begin with is attained externally by outside constraint, to the internalization of time discipline and to the imposition of self-discipline.[18] But this process of development occurs by including technological artefacts, which dictate temporal norms. These serve, on the one hand, to maintain and stabilize the time discipline introduced, but also lead to internalized feats of adaptation by including extra-somatic technologies. No society has done without the measurement of time and technologies, however rudimentary their structure, in the form of tools with which the structuring of space, time and social organization occurred.[19] But in pre-industrial societies, when not yet all time was the 'time of economics', it was neither necessary nor possible to keep people available for technological artefacts. People had to be available for the 'times of God' and for work. The rule of Saint Benedict, to which the first 'metronomic social system' in Europe is indebted,[20] provided for eight prayers which were distributed over the day and night and were preluded by peals of mechanical bells – a relatively externally controlled time discipline of punctuality and regularity, in other words, which moreover was valid only for a minority elite. Regularity which oriented itself by the mechanics of the even rhythm of machines also determined the time discipline which regulated the life of the bourgeoisie in the period of industrialization: a kind of social mechanics developed, which dictated the daily routine. 'The new bourgeoisie,' wrote Lewis Mumford,

> in counting house and shop, reduced life to a careful, uninterrupted routine: so long for business: so long for dinner: so long for pleasure – all carefully measured out, as methodical as the sexual intercourse of Tristram Shandy's father, which coincided, symbolically, with the monthly winding of the clock. Timed payments: timed contracts: timed work: timed

meals: from this period on nothing was quite free from the
stamp of the calendar or the clock. Waste of time became . . .
one of the most heinous sins.[21]

In contrast to the bourgeoisie, for whom the wasting of
time was of course detestable, but was still an open option,
the subjection to the time discipline of the machine was
inconceivably harsh for the workforce.

The machine offered a previously unknown availability
for purposes of industrial production and for the accumulation of profit, but equally demanded a previously
unrequired adaptation of the workers, who had no choice.
As a living appendage of the machine, they were tied to it,
initially without socio-political protective measures; indeed even the originally planned breaks were rigorously
suppressed. Increases in productivity, which become constant towards the end of the nineteenth century, essentially resulted from an improvement of technologies and
of the organization of the whole production process, but
also from an improved tuning of the behaviour of human
beings to the rhythms of the machine. Only gradually,
and always in a manner charged with conflict, were the
temporal norms of working-time regulations established
in a precarious balancing act between the internalization
of the work habit and the external necessity of social
existence in an industrial society.

Today, the social norms which refer to the time discipline of human beings are largely internalized and are
developing in dynamic interdependence with the temporal
norms built into technological artefacts. Acceleration, in
its continuing social transformation, does not just mean an
increase of speed in all social processes. It presupposes a
temporal norm of generally increased mobility, which is at
the same time the result of technologically and economically established processes of the conveyance of goods,
people, energy and information, which have to overcome
spatial and temporal distances. Thus mobility does not

remain confined to a technological specific, which can be optimized, i.e. realized in technological and economic terms. Instead, mobility is elevated to a socially dominant temporal norm, an assumed and striven-for social condition which is presupposed and hence expected, but is also to be regarded as the result of previous acceleration. Goods, people, energy, money and information are to change their position with increasing frequency, in order – in a comprehensive economic and cultural sense – to circulate. Being mobile has, in its social valency, assumed the meaning of mental and physical fitness for many people. The willingness for professional mobility is regarded as a prerequisite for remaining in the labour market and, skilfully handled, as a prerequisite for advancement in a successful career.

Social advancement is equated with social mobility, even though, strictly speaking, social decline is an equally probable form of mobility. International competition flourishes against a background of mobility, an immensely accelerated circulation of everything that is mobile or can be made mobile. Innovations and their dissemination promote mobility in the area of cultural production; it is not enough to innovate, since innovations have to be disseminated and this presupposes mobility. As always, when norms and social values are involved, an ideological distortion to maintain existing imbalances in power or to disguise the latter is never far away. In striking contrast to the expectations of mobility, for instance, which are entertained of the average employee, there are the key areas of political and economic power, which show astonishingly little mobility. Where, as in banking for instance, trust and familiarity with practices and discretion are presupposed, mobility is desired only in one's own closed sphere.

Another dominant temporal norm which was built into production technologies through its relation to economics and nevertheless became a generalized norm, indeed a social status symbol, is the shortage of time. This results

from the economic value it was given with capitalist accumulation and industrialization. Time was discovered as
a factor of productivity, and the economy is fundamentally
shaped to this day by questions of the economy of time.
Shortage of time became a central value in industrialized
societies – far beyond the area of production in all areas of
life. Making more of the time which is available and in
short supply is the supreme principle for technological
artefacts as well as for human activities. Rationalization
measures, the invention of the conveyor belt, the notori-
ous time and motion studies and other Taylorist prescrip-
tions for identifying wastes of energy and then eliminating
them, are only the most famous examples of the all-
embracing temporal norm of shortage, which people and
machines have to face and which is internalized in both –
in people by the rules which became a matter of course for
them and which manifest themselves in their being
'pressed for time', and in machines which can 'survive'
economically only when they are able to come to terms
with the shortage of time.

If the machine age is approaching its end today, or to
put it a better way, if machines and technological artefacts
have changed so much that they also contain other temporal norms than those which were fed into the old production technologies, then the newly added temporal
norm is that of flexibility. It finds its technological equivalent in the temporal availability that information-intensive
technologies have made possible, but also presuppose.
Information-intensive technologies have attained a new
quality of speed, which far exceeds that of human perception and the human ability to keep up. The moment it has
become technologically possible to carry out operations
and processes in 'nearly no time', the additional gain in
time becomes of marginal use. Through information-
intensive technologies, another law of the machine age is
also abolished, according to which worker and machine,
producer and consumer, transmitter and receiver had to

be simultaneously present. With the aid of new techniques of preservation and processing as well as storage, it has become possible largely to uncouple the acts of production and consumption not just in terms of place, but also in terms of time. Video recorders and stereo systems aid the consumption of cultural products independently of the moment of production, just as the techniques of preserving food have long since made it possible to eat fruits out of season. In the meantime, biotechnology is preparing the next preservation technique of temporal uncoupling: that which refers to the production and the use of living cells.

Temporal uncoupling, which extends from the older technologies of preservation in the case of food, via large areas of the production and consumption of services and cultural products with the aid of techniques of storing and processing information, to the biotechnological processes of the uncoupling of living organisms, helps the temporal norm of flexibility to attain a new, powerfully enlarged area of influence. As with other temporal norms, it is to be expected that it will also be culturally and socially diffused beyond the original area of production. Temporal flexibility, as well as the decentralization within the area of production which often goes along with it, will realize neither the utopian hopes nor wholly the fears, however, which are connected with the introduction of new technologies and a changed organization of work.

Every local decentralization presupposes a renewed form of centralization at a higher level. Every temporal flexibilization requires, with increasing complexity, new mechanisms in order to hold the seemingly loosening temporal connections together. Flexibility becomes possible against the background of a previously unattained degree of constant temporal availability, as the prerequisite and consequence of which it functions. Only the availability of people and their substitutes, technological artefacts, opens up the testing of new temporal patterns of uncoupling and coupling that can be optimized, which need the temporal norm of flexibility to legitimize them.

The extension of the temporal availability of technologies and human beings has already assumed visible and measurable proportions. Murray Melbin speaks of the 'colonialization of the night' and means by this the increase in nocturnal activities in American cities: New York does not sleep and neither does Boston, as can be seen from the frequency of crime, the number of admissions in the hospitals at night, but also the number of people who go to 24-hour supermarkets, bowling alleys and repair shops of all kinds. Many factories, but also post offices, newspaper editorial offices, hotels and hospitals work in three shifts; service industries like the fire brigade, key cutting service, places where one can get new nappies or insecticides, TV repair services and burial places, are on call day and night.[22] But the economic pressure of availability is also growing on the machines installed in the factories. If only because of the capital investment they contain, they have to run continuously, which leads to a distinct rise in shift-work. In the case of automated plants, the problem no longer arises, since they hardly require workers any more. Availability is automatically guaranteed.

What are above all 'ready on call' and continuously at hand are the electronic communication technologies, which have moved into offices and households. With the emergence of 'laboratory time' from the laboratory, now embodied in these technological artefacts, the patterns of temporal perception change once again. Other social structurings of time are needed in order to adapt to the demand for continuous attainability and to be able to use it.

Only gradually do temporal protective zones develop, so-called 'core times', in which presence or absence is demanded. Other technologies take on as substitutes the work of 'answering' and cause machines to speak with machines. But people will not be able to absent themselves as easily as the euphoric supporters of information technologies think. On the contrary. Other demands are made on their temporal availability; they have to react to the time-structures made possible in the new technologies by laboratory time, and structure them. New, collective and individual time-strategies in dealing with the new machine time, laboratory time, have to be developed. Technology is no longer to be found merely at work, no longer merely in the infrastructures like transport and energy systems, but everywhere, even in one's own house or, as with the mobile personal telephone, on one's own body. In the case of strategies for dealing with this, to be negotiated collectively, individual time-preferences therefore play a far greater role than was previously the case. But every time-strategy, however individually determined, bears within it the stamp of social time, for nobody can free himself or herself of the temporal patterns which connect him or her with others. The 'flexibilization' is a relative one. Here, too, time proves to be structure and structuring, and social time keeps on flowing through individual existence. The two following chapters are devoted to these themes.

The death of time, as a poetic and philosophical expression of the superseding of an epoch by another one, is itself a recurring theme which historians have called epochal consciousness.[23] To conceptualize this here means seeking to capture time by means of concepts: 'The concept lives on time. Its work consists in capturing the problem of development, fixing and shaping it.'[24] But neither the consciousness of change, nor capturing it by means of concepts, escapes the basic experience of repetition and of irreversible change, to which all aspects of time return. The repetitions which this epoch has set itself are those which stem from the production of what is always new – it is the process of innovation, which is accelerated with the aid of science and technology. But through the repetition aid of science and technology. But through the repetition which lies in the creation of what is new, the irreversible changes arise. The artificially created time of the laboratory, where under experimentally designed conditions nature is kept temporally present, leaves the laboratory, embodied in information technologies. This is also an irreversible process. It leaves options open – this is also the fundamental characteristic of the social constitution of time. The original myth of Cronos, as historians and anthropologists explain it, is in reality a creation myth. What is created is a concept of time, which in turn itself bears the historically social features of the society creating it.[25] The portrayal of the same myth at another time, and with other means of artistic expression, reflects at least as much very personal fears and ideas for overcoming them. Cronos's fear of the new age is understandable in view of what was then approaching in the way of acceleration and institutionalized willingness for constant, even though 'creative' destruction. The new age has kept on incessantly spewing forth its children ever since: the triumphal entry of laboratory time into society is one of its last up to now. The culture of science and technology dominant today finds other prerequisites and limitations in dealing with this, but it can look back on all previous experiences at the same time. Cronos does not have to devour his children a second time. But will the myth of creative destruction through innovation be sufficient to prevent it?

4

Politics of Time:
The Distribution of
Work and Time

... adults who have to be happy so that children can be happy.
We need time for this. We need time for an everyday life without
hustle and bustle. We need time for everyday culture. We need
time for the chance to be a public person. And we need time for
leisure. We do not need leisure time instead of a job, instead of
a family, instead of politics. We need it as surplus time.
                        Christiane Müller-Wichmann, *Zeitnot*

Nowhere does the desire of individuals to have more time
for themselves manifest itself as strongly and overwhelm-
ingly as in that time unit which itself became its temporal
reference point: in what is called everyday life. The change
which this concept has undergone reflects the change in
the quality of the perception of time which the latter has
experienced in the extended present. Everyday life – this
is no longer the merciless routine of a never-ending chain
of toil and drudgery, relieved solely by the temporal contrast, the temporary release symbolized by the holiday, the
Sunday.[1] Everyday life has shed the stasis of an ahistorical
permanence which was bestowed on it by a succession
of history-making turbulences, focused on other –
'Sunday' – events, or which a Eurocentric approach had
all too thoughtlessly ascribed to non-European societies.
Everyday life is the successful rehabilitation of the time of
'ordinary people', who have long since become the majority, in advanced industrialized countries at least. Everyday life is the temporal dimension of the welfare state, in

which it is institutions like those of social security that more or less effectively guarantee the temporal mastery of one's life-history – through school, health service and national insurance, including old-age pensions – but in which the smaller temporal units, the transitions from yesterday to tomorrow, with all their joys and cares, their formal and informal relations, are to be coped with by people themselves. This everyday life has long since devoured the Sunday, which became the weekend, but the weekend can be individually deferred and fixed on another day.

In the extended present, the festivals, the truly extraordinary times, have also shrunk and are solely to be found as archaic residues. Even the carnival, that game of inversions and of liberation from old certainties, that escape from reality into an orgiastic recreation of the cosmos,[2] now has to seek its moments in an extended present which can no longer afford to make longer periods completely free for games and tomfoolery, for a reversal of values and for disguises of all kinds. Everyday life still affords time for the so-called vicissitudes of life, but even here it is laid down how much time is to be expended on these: so many days off work in the case of a death; so many days off work for getting married; and so many for precisely defined vicissitudes of other kinds.[3]

Everyday life has become the bracket combining work and so-called free time; the private 'spending' of time and public spending form a new combination in everyday life. The great public institutions of the state and the economy, and their temporal perspectives, are confronted with the temporal perspectives of the citizens and employees, the economic subjects. In everyday life and all those private matters which become capable of being experienced, and thereby become a political issue, only through the conflict over the time they take up, the great changes are revealed concerning the quality of time itself, the valency attributed to it, and the exchange relations between quantity and

quality. The 'issues' at stake here have to do with increased demands on the quality of everyday life, with the
massive entry of women into working life and with the
different time culture which they bring with them. But it is
also a question of services which cannot be automated and
realized in the same way as the production of goods;[4] they
thus demand other temporal patterns which have to do
with informality, with the quality of human relationships
and with caring, and are based on other exchange relations
between time and money. The conflict over the reduction
in working hours, which Oskar Negt believes to be a
'political' struggle and not a mere wage conflict of a conventional kind,[5] still pre-eminently feeds off the traditional
notion of a uniform, continuous, predominantly male
working life, whereas the social reality of the labour
market has long since become 'unsteadied' and, in the
opinion of many authors, 'feminized'.[6] What is collectively
due for distribution, that for which a new politics of distribution has to be found, is work and time: work, because
the previous 'standard biography', given an increasing
tendency to participate in work and a stagnant social volume of available work, will be accessible only to a small
fragmentary group of the gainfully employed in future;
and time, because it is not least a question of a redistribu-
tion of paid and unpaid work between women and men.

The exchange relations between the public use of time,
that is spent with – paid – work, and the private, mainly
unpaid use, are distributed extremely unequally in society.
Publicly spent time, for the purpose of paid work, is an
important prerequisite for the fact that time can also be
spent privately. But it is easily overlooked that a good part
of time privately applied also represents an indispensable
prerequisite for its public use. The political aspect of
this is the exchange relation. To the extent that everyday
life is politically revalued, as time which belongs to the
citizens, and that their contributions to the general welfare are made politically apparent, demands arise. New

rights – everyday rights – become capable of formulation.[7] Time becomes the potential medium of exchange between quantity and quality of time, since in the extended present both have to be calibrated anew.

Time possesses the property that it can only be experienced as conflict, states Rinderspacher; in this it resembles health or justice.[8] Where it does not stand in contradiction to one's own desire, where the infringement of temporal standardizations is not subject to social, economic or psychological sanctions, time as such becomes incapable of being experienced. But the conflicts which make time capable of being experienced in this way are of very different origin in the constellations of power which spark them off and in the outlines of society presented as ideal in each case. In the analysis of the conflicts over time, if not before, it becomes clear that time represents a central dimension of power which manifests itself in the systems of time that dictate priorities and speeds, beginning and end, content and form of the activities to be performed in time. In the beginning, it was the priests who, in almost all societies, established the prevailing systems of time in accordance with those of the supernatural order, and separated sacred times from profane. Today, the systems of time are chiefly fixed by the market and the state. The market fixes times via the work to be done and the exchange relations between time and money. The state imposes its system of time via the legal system and thus structures the lives of its citizens. Standard biographies are created and legitimized, exceptions established. The law dictates biographical status – from when until when somebody is a child, a youth or an adult; which times are earmarked for military service or are given off for the birth and education of children; when the withdrawal from working life and going into retirement becomes obligatory. On the market, time is subject to the more universal medium of money with regard to the material and social range of its effect. Money can be accumulated and stored;

it can be pooled, saved and made to 'work' by earning interest, in order to be spent again at a later moment and in whatever partial amounts one likes. Time, if it is not a matter of working time which is invested for pension benefits, is 'wasted' if it finds no current use. In this respect, the 'rest period' of old age is pre-financed time. The money preference thus also predominates on the market. Money can be transferred directly and without respect of person, without being tied to demands on the interests and the motives, the spatial or temporal presence of givers and recipients. Time, on the other hand, remains tied to individuals and the context of their lives, to their biography and their abilities. The time of the ordinary worker or the secretary is 'worth' less than that of the boss, and it is not exchangeable at will. Only the market creates shortage of time via the universally prevailing scarce medium of exchange, money. The state, however, administers the shortage of time. Money is subject to no restrictions inherent in the medium. The nevertheless prevailing limitations on its use are social standardizations of what money is not allowed to do because it can do so much.[9] It is left to the state, however, to divide up over life the time scarce in life, but tied to individuals. It is the task of the state, as a successor to the church in the secularized area of national solidarity, to establish the time fixed for festivals and to determine when work has to 'rest'. The state draws up boundaries which mark off its territory from that of other states, but it also sets temporal limitations for its citizens: working-time regulations and hours of business, who is allowed to work at night for how long, for whom and for what reasons the clock may be stopped or 'put back'. In comparison with the money preference prevailing on the market, the state can merely intervene in a regulating and compensating fashion, if it is a question of 'crediting' periods, for instance, which have been spent on something other than work. On the market, any lack of time can be experienced as an incentive to improve the efficiency of one's lifestyle by an increased consumption of goods and services. The money preference predominates as a rule even when, or precisely when, the development of income and the job situation deteriorate, because then it becomes a question of defending both one's relative and one's absolute positions in the distribution of income. Status is determined by income and not by the extent of the free time available, as becomes clearly apparent from the example of unemployment. The time spent unemployed is compensated for only in the short term – and time without money proves to be economically worthless for most people.[10]

In view of the powerful temporal structuring of everyday life by the systems of time fixed and governed by the market and state, and in view of the structural changes which are leading industrialized societies out of the machine age and placing them under the temporal regime of the new technologies, it is thus no wonder that the politics of time per se has become a key strategic problem for otherwise very differently structured areas of politics. Changed methods of production and increased international competition demand regulations of time which are as flexible as possible. But new types of question of the distribution of time are also impending wherever the everyday life of women and men increasingly comprises both everyday working life and the so-called private sphere, in which the by no means so private requirements of family life are to be reconciled with the temporal regulations of gainful employment.

The different time cultures in which men and women move, and into which they have been socialized, here increasingly clash. The extended present of everyday life now refers to both sexes, but their time cultures are still differentiated along sex-specific lines. Questions of equality and the realization of social rights arise again wherever the unemployment situation threatens to become endemic, and whenever a not inconsiderable part of the population is not yet, no longer, or only temporarily and marginally anchored in the labour market. A new possessory title arises – the possession of a job; while in its shadow the number of those with no such possessions grows. What superficially presents itself in public as a discussion about a reduction in working hours conceals highly different sets of interests. Conflicts which are still hard to name, because they cannot easily be classified in conventional areas of politics, demand new social feats of integration and above all synchronization for which there are no conventional models. It is as if the machine age had 'flexibly unsteadied' itself, as it is called in the technical jargon for the new automated production technologies. It is as if the 'long arm of the job', which detained workers in physical and mental fatigue and dependence in the evenings and on holidays, and whose far-reaching effects on ways of life shaped by industrial production showed such strong tendencies to persist, is finally preparing to release people from its rigid routine, while the flexibly unsteadied job has not yet fully established itself. In the transitional period, there is a burgeoning, as so often, of the ideal projections and utopian blueprints of a society which 'appropriates time again', and which is to assure the individual of temporal self-determination. It is obvious that the old exchange relations between working time and free time, which are derived in their construction from the linear and 'continuous' working biography of the male employee, are no longer true. The quantity of free time cannot be uniformly transformed into the highly differen-tiated, neatly arranged demands for quality, derivable from subjective situations. Highly different ideas and meanings are subsumed under the concepts of working time and free time. Empirical investigations show that two desires predominate: the desire for a 'normalization' of one's own working time, which arises at the very moment when the supposed 'normal working time' ceases to be the compulsory model for reality; and the desire for 'temporal sovereignty', for the self-determined approach in dividing up and shaping working time in coordination and synchronization with other needs of life.[11] If in this connection the temporal conflicts are distinctly more perceptible to women, then it is because they have more powerfully contradicted the still conventional system of time, since their massive entry into working life, with their differently structured temporal needs. The empirical data further show how much more quickly the real working hours change than the ideas about them, but also what facts 'the terrible state of official working-time statistics' is able to conceal: on the one hand, the probably considerable overemployment of a section of employees in the face of a continuous process of structured mass unemployment; on the other hand, a process of unemployment which, according to all available data, is characterized by the cumulative dynamics of distribution of social inequalities in chances and risks of employment.[12]

Corresponding to the temporal availability which provides the technological framework for the new production technologies, there is a general temporal uncertainty in everyday life. The machine age is superseded by the pressure of a universal temporal availability via goods and services which are produced in changed conditions and equally demand to be consumed in changed conditions. For temporal availability is also to be found in the use of new products. Thus new periods of time literally open up – denser, more intensive ones, striving for continuous presence – which contain the potential for immensely more stress, as well as that for a complex temporal intensification in the present.[13]

In the production process, the machine is on the verge of replacing human beings. Its speed has already exceeded everything which could be got out of human beings by systems of increased performance, however ingenious they may be. Hence other principles of organization, which aim at optimal performance and efficiency in conditions of electronically controllable speeds, push their way to the fore. In the use of modern technologies of manufacture, for instance, the stock manufacture of big series of standardized products is replaced by short-term manufacture to order. The cushion of stocks is reduced and new principles of organization regulate the production processes. The rhythm of production is 'flexibly unsteadied'. Factory times and working times are uncoupled. The high capital intensity causes the management to use the factory 'right round the clock' as far as possible. Services and also a part of supply manufacturing, which are needed at irregular intervals to safeguard production but are to be furnished in synchronization with demand, are shifted outside. They turn into 'tertiary supply work'. With the largely automated loading of big containers, for instance, the organization of transport is such that it is possible – depending on the state of the financial transactions – to fix the place of sale and to direct the container there at the very last moment. So-called on-line systems provide that the actual act of production presupposes a skilfully planned optimizing organization, but one which is located outside in spatial terms and in manufacturing work. Production can then take place within the shortest time, but all other conditions, from financial calculations and storekeeping costs to supply operations, are located outside, but on call at any time. Flexible automation is merely the technological incarnation of flexible production methods, and the latter consist of a dense organizational network, linked by means of communication technologies, or small units and sub-units supplying work for one another. Economically valuable time is no longer lost because the worker is dawdling at the machine, but when there are costly waiting periods in an organization geared as synchronously as possible to optimizing time. Larry Hirschhorn has suggested the employment of highly specialized teams 'on call', who would have to rectify malfunctions. Apart from their highly specialized and complementary qualifications, they have to contribute nothing more than their temporal availability.[14]

Even though the form of organization described here comes closer to a high-performance flexibilization and cannot be regarded as typical of the whole area of production, it is the temporal principles of organization which clearly predominate: thus capital, raw materials or part-manufactured products and work are organized according to the financial, market and order situation, on the principle of short-term, and the most economical, temporal availability. Time is money, but money time is no longer to be found in the machine alone, but in a widely ramified, multi-layered, complex machinery of organization. It must be such that 'flexible' disposition and redisposition is possible at any time. Temporal disposability extends from venture capital via marketing to sales; the temporal network organizes the spatial one.

Production alone on the principle of optimal flexibilization is not yet enough. The products thus manufactured, above all the rapidly growing proportion of electronic devices, computers, fax and audiovisual technologies along with the relevant infrastructure, bring a part of the scientific laboratory time which has led to their development, as well as the temporal logic of industrial manufacture to which they owe their production, into working and everyday time. For their operation, their constant use and sale, similar temporal disposabilities are required to those which they already embody. The logic of temporal availability does not stop at industrial manufacture but spills over into other jobs and into so-called free time. A production process based on availability at any time of the necessary inputs as an optimizing principle demands as a correlate (free) time structures in which the time needed for consumption also manifests similar qualities to those built into technological products. Presupposing a class of buyers and users with a high income, consumption time must be such that things are usable in accordance with the built-in intention. But not just things – the proportion of consumption time reserved for individual production, for the do-it-yourself approach to products and individual services (if one thinks of those, for instance, which tend body and soul through therapy, massage and body-building), is also of the quality geared to availability at any time. In extreme cases this results, from a negative perspective, in a switch-on-and-off culture, in which temporal sequences follow one another arbitrarily, or temporal coincidences are correspondingly manipulable: the economic rationality which manifests itself precisely in the temporal sequence and synchronization of the production process is travestied, but not therefore abolished.

Conflicts are thus installed and to be met with almost everywhere. Between the time systems fixed by the market and the state, there are grey areas in which the working time of the black economy unofficially flourishes in conscious evasion of regulations to protect working hours and of tax laws. In the conflict over the reduction in working hours between employers and trade unions, in which far more is at stake than this alone, it will be up to the social welfare legislation of the state in the end to intervene with regulations. Against the background of the general money preference and the time preferences of male and female employees, highly individualized because dependent on their situation in life, no easily attainable solution emerges. But conflicts also arise in the immediate everyday life of all those who wish for more free time and more possibilities for shaping things at work, in order to attain that 'quality' of time which is intended to convey more autonomy, a reduction of the sense of strain, and more of the ability to structure time into meaningful, coherent units oneself. From an economic point of view, there is the permanent conflict which results from the opportunity costs and manifests itself in the dilemma between 'buying and do-it-yourself'. A socio-political conflict of larger proportions, and full of individual tragedy, results from unemployment, from involuntarily produced 'free time' and the extent to which work can be distributed 'more fairly'. Also full of conflicts is that area of general welfare in which the market and the state furnish public benefits in education, in health and through social services, which are paid for and for which one has to pay. Without voluntary and unpaid work, and this means the work and time of women, the present standard could not be maintained, however, and it will not be possible to sustain it in view of rising costs in the public sector. Thus it is a question here of the relationship between paid public time and private unpaid time. A separate private sphere, escaping the intervention of the state, no longer exists. And the hypothetical appeal to the forces of the market has been ideologically undermined; it is refuted daily by political reality. Public time has penetrated far into the private sphere, and private time can only be protected if it is made political. This occurs through women making demands in terms of the politics of time, when they insist on a new everyday culture and new everyday rights.[15] For in the temporal conflicts of women, all other lines of conflict between market and state, between working time and free time, involuntary and voluntary, paid and unpaid time, are expressed in exemplary fashion. Their conflicts result from the conflict-laden experience of a system of society and time, based on the division of labour, in which the time of men was never the same as the time of women. Thus different cultures of time have developed which go far deeper than pragmatic demands or attributed productivity would lead one to expect. The conflict breaking out here is a struggle for a new culture of time.

Every treatment of the subject of time never deals with time alone. The conflicts over time which are coming to light are strategic battlefields, political arenas, as the political scientists say, in which it is a question of better understanding what directions social processes are pursuing and

what options are open. Shifts in the patterns of the allocation of time, which are to be found in the historical
survey or in the international comparison, produce highly
meaningful chronograms of a society. So much time for
ourselves: so much time for others; so much time for work
(paid): so much time for work (unpaid); so much time
for buying: so much time for making; so much time for
fundamental needs: so much time for luxury; so much
time for waiting: so much time for getting things done.
The list of empirically ascertainable classifications can be
refined, and continued almost at will. Every categorization
says something about the content and its quality at the
same time, since the assessment results from the relation
with the remaining pattern of allocation. Desires and
reality can be confronted with one another, classified according to the features of the stratification of a society.
Retrospectively, it is possible to 'estimate' what social
development has changed and what it has 'brought'.

The empirical data for such an analysis are available in
their rudiments, but fragmented and tied to local patterns
of inquiry as the calendars and calculations of time in
medieval towns once were. Thus here is just one example
of a historical change in the social allocation of time,
empirical findings which, like all others, are open to interpretation. The extension and gradual reduction of
working hours underwent a dramatic development in
Europe from the beginning of the machine age on. In
Germany, for instance, the ten- to twelve-hour day, which
prevailed around 1800, rose to eleven to fourteen hours in
1820. In the period between 1830 and 1860, that period
in which the first statutory reduction was achieved by the
labour movement in England in the form of the Ten-Hour
Bill, working hours in Germany grew to fourteen to sixteen hours.[16] Sundays and holidays were lost in many
cases, and weekly working hours shot up accordingly. The
turning point occurred only with socio-political legislation
around 1870.

Since then, with international time differences, there has been a series of relevant developments everywhere in Europe. General life expectancy has risen thanks to improvement in the control of epidemics, in the sewerage system and hygienic conditions, in medical progress and the development of a public health system. Child labour, which was widespread in the nineteenth century, was drastically reduced at the beginning of this century, prohibited, and replaced by attendance at state schools. The view prevailed that human labour was able to accomplish more if children went to school, instead of prematurely wearing themselves out with work, and that through an improved state of health in the population its output generally rose. The welfare state, with its social welfare legislation and institutions for social security, was able to establish itself as the historical 'project of the century'. Only around the middle of the present century, however, were the public institutions for education, health and social services so far established, had the need for additional workers in the labour market so far increased, that women began to enter the labour market and paid work in massive numbers. This development is conveyed in a series of figures in which working time is expressed in the form of years of working life.[17] According to these figures, up to 1871 in the UK, a male worker spent almost 56 years of his life working; around 1950, it was still 50.9 years; only in 1981 did this fall to 46 years. Thus the progress of a whole century can also be gauged by the fact that the male section of the population gained ten years free of work. Like all statistics, these also not only conceal individual differences, but ignore what happened in the way of historical events, wars or colonial expansion. For women, the picture appears complementary. At any rate, they appear as historical subjects in the official statistics as early as 1871, even though only that part of their life is recorded as working time which they spent in the labour market for bad remuneration. At the beginning of the period under consideration here, this was almost twenty years of life, a figure which remained more or less constant, with fluctuations, up to the 1950s, to rise continuously since then. Up to 1981, English women spent thirty years of their lives on paid employment outside the home. In another English investigation into the working life of men and women who were facing retirement, the author comes to the conclusion that a *de facto* alignment of male and female working careers is beginning to emerge. The working-time conditions of both are becoming fragmented and discontinuous, occupational social decline is increasing, the proportion of part-time work is rising and with it the marginal status in the labour market, retirement age is showing increasingly large variations, and ambiguities in status are rising among those not officially regarded as employed. All this against the background of a development in which the total duration of working life is beginning to approach that of non-working life, for after the deduction of working life there remain to men and women on average just as many years which they do not spend working: almost three decades.[18]

Almost – but before jubilation breaks out over the time gained, and this is muted anyway if one takes into account the microstructure of economic conditions in which the majority of older people, and above all of older women, have to live, it is worth considering the historical time sequence again. For if the statistical average of years of life is ascertained, as Ausubel and Grübler have done, a striking constant emerges: if the official working life of women and men is added up and followed over the period of a hundred years, then despite the rise in life expectancy and the later entry into working life, despite time-saving household technologies and early retirement, nothing has changed. Human working life, if human is taken to mean that of women and of men, constantly amounts to thirty-eight years of life over the period of a hundred years.[19]

Of course, it can be immediately speculated here that such a constant expresses the 'necessary' amount of time which a society requires in order to preserve itself, where the level of 'self-preservation' is variable. But such speculations are idle, particularly if a freely available 'residual time' is to be deduced from them. The machine age was, at any rate, directed towards the exploitation of all available reserves of time. Life was divided into those two areas described by Marx and others: the time for production, which was spent at the machine, and the time of reproduction needed for the mental and physical restoration of the capacity for work. Given the far shorter life expectancy and the minimal time at school in comparison with today, there were no reserves of time for the overwhelming majority of the population: few for old age, and almost none for what is called free time or consumer time today. Women were integrated into the production process above all before they were married, and had to shoulder the main burden of the urgently needed work of reproduction in their families. Thus what is concealed by an artificially constructed constant like that of the thirty-eight years of human work has to be seen in the context of more comprehensive changes.

One of these concerns the status of work in the nineteenth century, and that given to the concept of free time in the twentieth century. For the political thinkers of the nineteenth century, as well as for the activists of the labour movement, work was regarded as the source of economic wealth, as an essential human need. If the social struggle was conducted in terms of the demand for the 'right to work', then this meant a declaration of the right to share in economic surplus value, of the right to work which served the development of human beings and their abilities, and which did not run counter to the idea of satisfaction, but promoted it. Work was to be 'redeemed', via the radical changes in social relations. Whereas the twentieth century is still governed, one is tempted to say, by the hope for free time, though whether 'the miracle of liberation from totally being taken up with work'[20] will ever become a reality, whether the time 'released' will become a source of freedom, emancipation and self-realization, or whether it is merely a question of an illusion, the destruction of which is followed by fresh hopes, remains a basic topic for social reflection.

The fact that the desire for more free time became overpowering, in view of the burden of working time even in terms of pure quantity, is understandable. But where does the time 'released' come from? Part of it may have been wrested from the employers by the labour movement in a dogged struggle, always in conjunction with technological improvements and a rationalization of organization based on the division of labour, which led to increases in productivity. Another part of it stems from women's previously invisible reserves of time, which were not officially identified and represented 'social free time' in the calculation of human working life, even if it was devoted to unofficial, unpaid work. One part, however, paradoxically results from the sheer extension of the need for time which was introduced into the history of humanity with the machine age: the need for time for production, but also the need for time for the consumption of what is produced. In advanced industrial societies, a further increase in efficiency is not just a prerequisite in the area of industrial production, but time also has to be shaped, organized and rationalized more efficiently in order to be able to consume the goods and services produced for consumption. Time is needed and used up in order to produce and to destroy what is produced, in order to make room for new products and services, but also in order to be able to maintain and reproduce the conditions for continued production and continued consumption.

The necessity of creating time for consumption is already contained in the cycle of innovation, repetition and obsolescence. Consumption can occur in many kinds of ways. Just as it is possible to gobble down food in a fast food restaurant or to be cosseted by a *chef de cuisine* in a splendid ambience, the setting for the consumption of products and services which come on the market can also be shaped in very different ways – but it always needs time. One of the first thinkers to refer to this was Paul Lafargue, the son-in-law of Karl Marx. In his book *The Right to Laziness*, published in 1883, he advanced the theory that the bourgeoisie had to proceed from its industriousness to idleness, because industrial society was dependent not just on producers, but also on consumers.[21] And Georges Bataille, in an essay written in 1933 on the 'concept of spending', comes to the conclusion that there is no society which does not produce surplus value, but nor is there one which does not also devote a large part of its time, goods and energies to unproductive expenditure, indeed to wastefulness: 'Terrible as human misery is, society has never been able to control it to the extent that the striving for self-preservation, which gives production the semblance of a purpose, has outweighed the striving for unproductive expenditure.' Bataille further concludes that every society has to cope with two main problems: production which serves the preservation and propagation of the species and which represents the starting point for the development of every social system, and the consumption and destruction of surplus production and energy; for this forms the reaction to the problems arising from growth.[22]

The theory of 'necessary annihilation', the analysis of the modes of destruction which societies choose in order to destroy their surplus products, just as the Indian tribes on the north-west coast of America once did in their institutionalized festivals of wastefulness, the potlatches, draws attention to extreme forms of consumption, the most extreme of which is surely war. But annihilation does not necessarily require a lot of time. What requires time, time for consumption, is more probably slow wastefulness, the forms of that which Veblen once described as lavish expenditure in the allocation of time for consumption by the sophisticated middle classes. But mass production also brought with it mass consumption. The fear of 'mass leisure', which sparked off countless investigations of leisure in which it was implied that the class enjoying 'leisure' for the first time was incapable of leisure, is a special chapter in the history of cultural hypocrisy.[23] Even though this fear has not been completely overcome, particularly with reference to the passive consumption of mass media, the initial position still looks different today.

The extent, structure and intrinsic quality of time free for consumption follow from what is produced and from the working conditions in which it is produced. 'The long arm of the job' still continues to reach into life, of course, but it becomes longer and more mediated. How time free for consumption is spent today, what is done in it and how, has resulted from two initial conditions: from one's own working conditions and from the nature of consumer goods and services, i.e. of that which others produce. They bear within them their built-in 'time', which makes certain temporal demands on all those who want to consume them. Where the work processes can be temporally un-coupled, optimized and above all intensified, the same will also be true of the chosen leisure activities. Where consumer goods bear within them their built-in, pre-produced and programmed complexity for the self-development of the user, where every kind of sport has its own outfit, kit, and practice and journey times, where every hobby insists on assuming a professional character and together with free time a 'lifestyle' and a corresponding feeling are propagated, consumption becomes the mimicry of pro-duction and cannot do much more than follow the given times. It used to be the content of work, its duration and burden, which moulded – in an immediate and un-protected manner – the remaining time, which was pre-eminently experienced as time free from work. What could be done in it was, like a cruel parody, dictated by work, for which the content and the structure of free time were only able to fulfil a compensatory role. Today, it is admittedly still one's position in the hierarchy of income and qualifications in the labour market, and the job patterns connected with it, which are dominant in the choice of freedom of consumption and its activities, but these are joined by the mediation via consumer goods and by the time structures built into it. The time for consumption becomes independent as part of a comprehensive process of social differentiation. But unlike the potlatch and other festivals which were held in tribal and agrarian societies, the festivals in industrial societies are rationed in terms of time and mostly of brief duration. They tend to become everyday routine themselves, which then sparks off the desire for new festivals which are themselves soon submerged in everyday routine again. In contrast also to the former alternation between maximum labour intensity and idleness, resulting from a primarily task-oriented division of time which had imposed on agrarian societies an irregular system of time adapted to the rhythms of nature, the tendency today is rather to extend labour intensity to the idleness which has become time free for consumption.

But alongside the time for production and consumption, there is the time for interpersonal services. The shift in the allocation of time between public, paid time and private, unpaid time, however, and the political conflict over their exchange relation, become understandable if the role of the state is analysed as well, which has entered into the division of labour between the sexes. For the establishment and consolidation of the welfare state, which is here taken to be synonymous with a socio-political system that recognizes many forms of expression in concrete historical terms, work was and is the central, integrating mechanism holding the institutions of social security together. It is status in the labour market, when, for how long, in what capacity, and with what breaks somebody is employed, which determines whether and to what extent he or she is entitled to draw the benefits of the social security system in cases of illness, accident, unemployment and old age. It is the already paid, pre-financed time in the labour market which decides who – as in the cases of insurance claims just mentioned – is permitted to draw time with payment, yet without work. For those who were not included in this work-insurance system, not even through their family affiliation above all to a male employee, remedial measures developed which, as a continuation of the old poor relief, were always conceived merely as a safety net. The original aim of the welfare system was rooted in making means of subsistence available whenever income was lost for recognized reasons, that is, when either the labour market or the informal safety net of the family failed. In a second stage of the development of the welfare state, which did not occur until the 'three golden decades' after the middle of the present century, the state, with a rapid increase of public expenditure, took charge of the development of the tasks of reproduction which had been performed within the family at an earlier, rudimentary and still little-differentiated stage. Education, health and social services were now developed, professionalized and expanded on a governmental level. No longer just those who have a status in the labour market are now entitled to receive benefits, but everyone is now given new 'social rights' on the strength of their universal status as citizens of the state.

In this phase, women begin to enter public life and the labour market in increasing numbers for the first time. The welfare state itself becomes the largest employer of women through the newly created possibilities of gainful employment. Not only is the burden on women eased by professional helpers, teachers, doctors, social workers and therapists, but they take up these professions themselves. Above all in northern countries, women begin to become aware of their double status as employees and citizens. It becomes increasingly more apparent that women shoulder the main burden of invisible and unpaid work, which is indispensable to the public welfare system. It also becomes apparent that women, by virtue of their different situation in life, have different time preferences from men; they desire more time, whereas men desire more money; women press for a reduction in the working day, while men tend to prefer a longer annual holiday. They begin to express these preferences and to oppose their interests to those of corporate organizations. As citizens, they demand not just 'time for work', but also 'time for everyday life', for those tasks which they fulfil in multiple ways in their supposedly private time.[24]

With the welfare state undertaking tasks of reproduction and services which were formerly fulfilled within the family, even though on a smaller scale, neither in a specialized nor in a professionalized manner, patterns of time entered public gainful employment which cannot automatically be adapted to those of industrial production. Even if the lessons in schools are thoroughly standardized in terms of form and content, and even if hospitals or old people's homes may be regarded as 'factories' for patients in many respects, the periods of time furnished there and devoted to nursing cannot be rationalized, automated or made flexible in the same way as they can for the new production technologies. Not yet – for the pervasion of personal services with new communication technologies, the computerization of hospitals and social services, is imminent. There still remains a period of interaction with patients or clients, however, which cannot easily be handled via machines, a balanced negotiating process of the giving and taking of time. Peter Pritchard, one of the few doctors who have tackled the problem of time as a form of interaction between doctors and patients, argues for a participatory orientation 'that is not popular with professions, but is slowly gaining ground'.[25] It is a question here of more than a better use of waiting periods. But even if doctors and others learn to budget their time better through better organization and a change in their personal habits in their lives and work, there still remains a stubborn residue: a period of inter-human caring, furnished in the form of a service which cannot be replaced totally by technology, or totally by monetary calculation, or by organization, however skilful it may be; a residue of time freed of financial charge as the exchange medium of human relations which – still – resists, in its irreducibility and universality, the general exchange medium of money and its dominance on the market. There are residues of relations in which time can only be exchanged for time, and in which the norm of reciprocity determines the prevailing tone of human gatherings. But it can be seen that time in which empathy, affection and solidarity can be expressed only through personal presence is on the retreat, that new conventions are establishing economically acceptable exchange relations, when time becomes replaceable by money and technology, and by purchased substitutes. Personal presence becomes a partial one with the aid of technological communication – the voice on the telephone, the electronically transmitted word, the instantaneous but indirect communication, replace the complete person. What remain are archaic remnants of an exchange relation in which time could only be traded for time, and the mediation of purchased replacement time via money did not yet exist. All time of caring, occasions for mutual joy or mourning, time which is qualitatively tied to particular individuals, retains traces of these archaic remnants, but they are simply remnants.

In the everyday routine of the welfare state, the human time of services presents itself in a much more banal fashion, of course. In recent years, private forms of organization, unpaid voluntary work, and informal networks have increasingly also become a theme of government social policy.[26] Patients and clients are being discovered as 'partners' of professional helpers and by professionally operating institutions. Their time is an important resource for furnishing one's own services and self-help. Under the pressure of falling social security benefits, a corresponding revaluation of all informally usable resources occurs which ultimately return to the resource of unpaid, private time. Laura Balbo has employed the image of crazy quilts in this connection, that patchwork of colourful remnants stitched together by American pioneer women in their remaining free time. In exactly the same way, women also use their remaining time today to furnish those services at home, in schools and clubs, in hospitals, neighbourhoods and offices, which are regarded as private.[27]

In the labour market, the general preference for money predominates over the preference for time; what people do in their private time is interpreted as the desire of consumers. To the extent, however, that the boundaries between public and private are beginning to become blurred in everyday life, by formerly private time becoming public since it invades public space and publicly paid (working) time, new – political – questions arise about a fair distribution of work and time. All stated preferences for working time are preferences related to certain phases of life and situations. They are dependent on sex and age, one's family situation, income and class affiliation. And to the extent that people's biographies, conditioned by the general work situation, become more unsettled, the time preferences are also exposed to larger fluctuations. They become transitional preferences.[28]

Analysis of the conflicts and of the difficult negotiations over reduction in working hours falls short if they are seen merely as an extension of the previous conflict, and not as much more fundamental questions of distribution and organization. The extension of public time and public space into what was formerly called the private sphere is increasing – technologies are crossing this boundary as well as the interdependences just described between cases of unpaid free time furnished for purposes of general, public welfare. In this way, private everyday life becomes more public, becomes part of the market and the state, and emerges from its former anonymity and political protective coating. As consumers and female citizens, people demand new rights and seek to have a hand in shaping the political processes which intrude on their everyday lives. The politics of working time and the politics of living time are closely connected, and they are linked with one another via the labour market and social policy. The current model of the labour market is still based on rights, incentives and achievements derived from a continuous, lifelong and full-time working biography. This normal case has ceased to be the norm, though, just as normal working hours have long since become abnormal, and in the Federal Republic of Germany only a quarter of all households correspond to the popular notions of a normal family – parents with children.

But that is not all. Even the public health sector and the state-run social services are getting into difficulties in the face of a demographic shift which is drastically increasing the proportion of the elderly, and cost increases which are connected with the technologizing of medicine and the equal rise in expectations and demands. 'Care', writes Martin Lagergren in a study of the allocation of time by professional helpers in the Swedish welfare system, 'is above all a question of time spent by somebody for somebody else.' The study has calculated, by means of a simulated model, that the limits of financial feasibility will soon be reached.[29] What then? Where is the unpaid, urgently needed time to come from? Are measures in which the state taxes the 'free time' of its citizens, just as income is taxed now, the solution, or is it to be found in the horrific vision of a fully automated hospital, with electronically connected home-care services which transmit the nurse's smile via a screen?

The concept of 'free time' conceals what political options are open. On the market, depending on income, the option arises of buying or of do-it-yourself. Through the universal medium of exchange, money, all allocations of time are left up to the consumers. In the area of state politics, it is a question of working out options which mediate between the politics of living time and the politics of working hours, between the unattainable ideal of life-long full employment for all and an extremely fragmented employment situation of part-time jobs, in which the employees are at the mercy of the employers without trade union protection and are discontinuously employed. It is a question of finding a balance between the divergent interests and time preferences of women and men, but also between the expanding conflicts of interests of the corporately organized trade unions and the desire of women for more part-time jobs. The questions of the distribution of work and time under discussion here turn out to be difficult in several respects. The status and the rights derived from one's position in the labour market always turn out to be stronger than the universal status of an ordinary female citizen. New difficulties arise from the lack of a generally applicable set of criteria for the quality of the time under discussion. Time is translatable into money, but the same quantity of time means something very different for those who live in different circumstances or who have different possibilities of shaping their time. Viewed in this light, the purely quantitative factor of time stemming from the machine age has been joined by a qualitatively organizational factor, which has long since overshadowed the purely quantitative one. It is one thing to perceive the nature of time, its valency and social setting, in a discriminating fashion; it is another to meet the different political demands on its organizing capacity for coping with everyday life. In both cases, however, time has ceased to be a private matter. What are the prospects of solving the conflicts presented here? In a detailed analysis from the strategic viewpoint of active participants, Helmut Wiesenthal comes to some striking conclusions. Most serious of all is probably the empirically established conclusion that there is no general time preference in the sense that a larger group of employees desires 'more time' and is prepared to sacrifice portions of income for it.[30] There are limited time preferences, against the background of a surprisingly broad spread of actual working hours, but they cannot be reduced to a common denominator. Even the influence of monetary trade-offs is limited: almost three quarters of those asked prefer the present relation between time and money. Wiesenthal infers from this an approximate satiation of the relative need for free time. A reversal is possible, of course, but the conditions in which it could occur are narrowing: there would have to be precise objectives like the earlier demand for the eight-hour day; real income would have to rise continuously for a while in order to create the need for more time for spending money; more attractive uses of free time or so-called income-substitute activities, like working in one's own garden, which presuppose no additional need for income, would have to be offered. This results in a pessimistic outlook for the chances of a re-standardization of the divergent patterns of working time. Since the present initial position of the working-time situation is extremely divergent and unequal, a levelling up could only be carried out via individually specific changes in working time. This, in turn, encounters considerable difficulties. The more concretely the patterns of distribution of working time aimed at are defined, the smaller the segment of employees becomes which sees its preferences realized in them. From the multitude of articulated time preferences, not a single one appears capable of social generalization any more.

The situations at work and in life seem to have moved into a state of temporal flux. The experience of temporal systems changes with one's situation in life, and the perception of time becomes a dependent variable. In a situation in which there have to be frequent changes between different jobs, situations in life and spheres of life, the decisive standpoint of individual orientations also changes more easily. And yet, in such a situation in life and at work, marked by deep temporal uncertainty, the desire grows all the more powerfully to have the right of disposal and possession of something which itself has to remain available: proper time.

Viewed in terms of society as a whole, a paradoxical structural convergence of patterns of time arises, in which uncertainty strives for new order. The area of industrial production is characterized by a comprehensive phase of rationalization for the reorganization of industrial manufacturing. Flexible manufacturing systems simultaneously facilitate special and mass production; through so-called 'just in time' organization, a close adaptation of production to a demand that is becoming more sophisticated can be made through computer-based networking of processing stages with one another, and of the temporally optimized delivery by suppliers. The extended technological and organizational possibilities are geared to optimization that is economical in terms of cost and time, but they increase the patterns of combination between human presence and mechanical processes. Whether and how far these new possibilities of combination, which permit an emancipation from formerly rigid practical constraints, are passed on to employees is an open question which will be decided politically.[31]

The other extreme is dominated by patterns of time which, because it is mostly a question of unpaid time tied to individuals and connecting individuals, are not yet under the same pressure of rationalization. It is the temporal availability – at any time – in service time which is used by people for people. Even though we cannot totally abstract here from the marginal economic conditions of the possible substitutability of individuals by technologies or other paid helpers, there *are* optimizing strategies. The child who can be alone only in the presence of his or her mother, who has to remain in sight in order to be supervised, and the mother who combines this supervision with countless, overlapping 'secondary' activities which simultaneously come up in household routine, with countless interruptions again and again, are used to a 'flexibilization' of their daily time in another sense, which is not yet fully rationalized in economic terms. The doctors whom Peter Pritchard advises to organize their time in such a way that, if necessary, they can also find time for their dying patients, would equally be living a flexible and optimizing routine, oriented towards being on call, while not totally caught up in the money nexus.

For all the stubbornness of time, however, which cannot yet be fully substituted by money, in which something is still left of the natural currency of time for time, and which is subordinated to a norm of reciprocity based on this, a process of structural alignment still takes place between the two patterns of optimizing and flexibilization: the approximation to economic calculation. Of course, it is the mixed forms which will make the way there a long and complex one. The time of professional helpers is valuable, and a considerable portion remains of contributions to be made by oneself. The user-friendly omnipresence of communication technologies invites a more efficient shaping and more efficient mixing of the time of both. Partial solutions dominate any total solution. But the final exchange relation is dictated by the market, is fixed by the universal medium of exchange, money. The natural currency of time for time remains an endearing form of archaic convention, a residual ritual of social existence. It is not to be wholly ruled out, but is destined to be an exception. It already belongs to the other, 'sacred' time which is withdrawn from economically structured processes for a brief period. It retains a value which cannot be precisely specified in economic terms, but for this very reason it becomes more valuable, because it is rarer. Thus the law of economics – scarcity – is confirmed even where it is deprived of its phenomenon. Because a few moments of human time are able to escape the money nexus, they receive a significance which makes them unmistakable. Thus time receives its temporarily valid individuality. Paradoxically, as a Western obsession, it can be realized precisely when Western rationality and rationalization subject all time to the anonymity of market relations and their mutual capacity for substitution. At this very moment there arises a new claim precisely to this time: the claim to proper time. Is this claim also just an illusion?

5

The Longing for the Moment

Im ein ani li, mi li?
Ouk'she ani, lei atsmi, ma ani?
Weim lo ashar, ei ma tai?

If I am not for myself, who is for me?
If I am for myself, what am I?
If not now, then when?

Mishnah, Sayings of the Fathers

Probably never before have so many people simultaneously experimented with time as they are doing today. For many, the experiment is involuntary. With the wristwatch, made in Hong Kong, from where 590 million of them are exported each year, a further piece of Western rationality enters people's minds and social structures which previously lived their own local time and were attached to other structures of time. In Western industrialized countries, escape attempts are being tested, where the pressure of time is intensifying, and uchronias invented which are intended to lead out of Western time. In the different cultural quality of Eastern mysticism and its sense of time, people consciously search for other experiences of time, for an escape from everyday stress, through meditation and relaxation, through rebirth or stopping the moment. It is not just that the West has pervaded other cultures with its economy of time; the gods there have also become mobile, and the Buddha of the three times drops in wherever he is invoked. But most experiments are less exotic. They take place in the area of conflict between, on the one hand, the individual endeavour to be able to realize a fraction of proper time, to structure the time available into meaningful units and to be able to optimize it towards one's own everyday needs, and on the other hand the necessity of coping, at a social level, with the limitations contained in the extended present. Meaningfully appropriating proper time is dependent on the – unequal – initial social position, on the social hierarchies of power and income, in which people find themselves. Comprehending the limitations of the extended present, and managing to deal with them, awaits individual and collective solutions; it seeks answers which a scientific and technological culture gives to the problems it has created itself. This, reduced to a bare common denominator, is what is concealed by the slogan about the 'quality' of time, which goes beyond the demand for quantity.

'Time as such is not scarce. The impression of the scarcity of time arises only from the overtaxing of experience by expectations. Experiences and actions need time and can therefore be accommodated in a given span of time only in a limited fashion. The horizon of time and the structure of expectation must therefore be brought into line', so runs the sociologist's prescription.[1] For the economists, on the other hand, the rise of the 'hurried leisure class' of grafting managers who have almost everything, only no time, automatically and axiomatically follows from the rising standard of living. 'I work so hard that I am killing myself and ruining my family. But I am earning so much that I can afford it', so runs one of the concise summaries.[2] From this viewpoint, it is the so-called 'opportunity costs' which arouse the hunger for time. With the increase in productivity, it becomes more costly not to work, and time is calculated according to what could have been earned if a person had worked – considerations which admittedly presuppose that work and earnings are there. In order to cope with the 'shortage of time' or the 'hunger for time', there are very different strategies. The problem is different for organizations and for managers, and different again for working mothers, who are all dependent on time in varying and unequal ways.

Under pressure of time, as Luhmann shows, shifts of preference occur in the long term within organizations, in favour of what is scheduled and restricted, i.e. the selection of factual arrangements and value judgements ultimately changes in accordance with the establishment of temporal priorities. The pressure of time facilitates the 'institutionalization of opportunist pursuit of values'. This means that, in a social system which has attained a high degree of complexity and variability in the achievement of values, it becomes useful to break up conflicts of values – say between such different values as life, hygiene, entertainment, peace, culture, freedom or provision for old age – into a temporal succession. This robs them of something of the antagonistic harshness of a struggle for survival. A decision is then needed only about immediate priorities; the adherents of other values are not discredited, they just have to – wait. Time can also be saved through trust and routine, and through artificially set deadlines otherwise impeded tasks can be raised into the protective zone of the urgent and restricted.[3] Managers who work in organizations which set deadlines for them, and who are expected to set deadlines for others, attempt for their part to cope with the chronic lack of time. Every hour in the appointments diary is organized by secretaries or assistants, whose task it is to negotiate, buy and sell their boss's time. All agreements reached are ultimately – finely coordinated with the hierarchy of the status system – only tentative. If new priorities arise, the appointments have to be altered, postponed, rescheduled. It is as if time would do anything to escape the straitjacket which is to be put on it.[4]

The higher the status hierarchy, the more tentative the commitments become, for only the time of subordinates can be firmly determined in advance and assigned. The managers themselves suffer from chronic lack of time and constantly try to do too much. By means of all sorts of tricks, they intensify and delegate, they use even faster means of communication and attend to even more jobs at the same time, in order to gain time in this way. But ultimately even their – long – working day remains limited. The abundance of what still remains to be done, and the possibilities which cannot be realized, far exceed what can be fitted in, however well their time is organized.

Christiane Müller-Wichmann has rightly complained, in irritation and anger, that it is always also a question of taking into account the chance of disposing of remaining residues of time, in order not to lose sight of the 'unequal access to time'. For managers and other

> favoured groups of people, despite their quantitative burden, are nevertheless capable of largely structuring their time themselves. Because they are able, as it were, both to increase time and to make free time in the first place from empty remnants, they are presented with possibilities which women above all do not have, the organization of whose time is either strictly laid down or extremely fragmented, so that the available remnants of time cannot be assembled into meaningful free time.[5]

The problem of the unequal availability of proper time arises again here. But despite these striking differences, the feeling of the lack of time in the face of the wealth of alternative possibilities – of consuming, of working, of living – is spreading in general. Every decision which is made is a destroyed possibility. Above all through modern means of communication, people have become more aware how else they might spend their days or hours. They therefore experience the lack of time more clearly. Whenever they concentrate on a piece of information, they deny themselves the possibility of fully concentrating on another one. 'They are more aware of other places in the world where they might be, with other men, or other women, at other meetings, at other conferences, at other exhibitions, on other trails, reading other books, on other moonlit nights.'[6]

In view of these findings, and many more could be cited, it is not surprising that people have been seized by the longing for a differently lived time. The desire to 'work differently', which also resonates in the public debate about a reduction in working hours, is at the same time a vehicle of the longing for a time which can be structured differently, and which promises an escape from everyday routine and the realization of at least a fraction of those possibilities which is thwarted by the actual expenditure of time. A new departure – but where to and how? Here the paths to Uchronia begin to fork. Both have long since ceased to exist, the remote places, and the fictitious, distant future, created despite temporal discontinuities, in which the ideal society can be outlined, and which can be dreamed about 'as a compensation for the present misery, in social, political, moral, and literary terms, whatever the sensitive heart or enlightened reason may desire'.[7] Uchronia is now, and it too seeks realization in the extended present.

The first path leads straight into the Cockaigne of full time. If sausages once dropped from the sky in this imaginary land for people racked with famine to eat their fill, then the modern dream of the temporal paradise is full of the magic formula 'if only I had time for . . .'. The imagination can then run riot, since only two conditions are to be met for the fulfilment of all the wishes it produces: to have more time and, if possible, money too. The poor wish for the means of transport of the rich, and all their luxury in the way of time and money; the fans of free time want to make their pleasures, in which they are led to believe by a uchronically well-versed advertising industry, instantaneously and simultaneously realizable, and contemplative people want a bit of ecologically clean eternity. All want to appease their hunger for time, without ever becoming thirsty again; they want to live faster, more fully, without therefore arriving earlier or empty. More free time: less work; more consumption: more fun; more in the way of life: living differently; so the short formula might run with variations.

The second path to Uchronia is far more sophisticated. It is the path richest in tradition, burdened and laden with the toil of the oppressed in a world ruled by lords and masters. What has shifted is the temporal emphases. The suffering from time, from which uchronia promises liberation, is no longer the twelve- or sixteen-hour day, but the increasing labour intensity, the negative time stress, and above all the lacking temporal autonomy of one's own availability. Attempts to attain a reduced intensification, to counter the economy of time with its 'ecology', to bring work 'to life' – all this struggling in words for the 'reappropriation of time', of which people were collectively and individually robbed by industrialization, has the contemporary familiar ring of a discourse in which 'only the utopias are real' (Oskar Negt) and which has now also discovered time.[8] Autonomy and self-determination, temporal flexibilization in the interests of employees, new forms of distribution of working time and living time, are recurring themes which seek to oppose the constraint of time, to remove it and replace it with the dream of self-determination.

The third uchronia seeks to 'liquefy frozen time again', to make time die again in order to approach other ideas of time 'in the shadow of a catastrophic end of time'.[9] It feeds on ideas which start from a change in temporal rhythms and strive for a new balance between the linearity of mechanized and homogenized time and the unexpected element, the spontaneity of the 'vicissitudes of life'. The argument is directed towards a resumption of natural rhythms; the hundred-year-old battle against nature is to be brought to an end and homeostasis replaced by homeorhythmics.[10] Linearity is not to be totally abolished, but human routine is to be broken, and shaped in a less regular fashion. The force of habit which gives stability to social life and represents the preservative and conservative

aspect of society – since 'hardly anything is more conservative than the habitualized behaviour with which one
inhabits everyday life'[11] – is to blend with what is new and
unexpected, the breaking of routine, which also stands
for linearity. The reintroduction of cycles is intended to
signal not just repetition, but also the impetus of a new
line. The third uchronia has concrete proposals in store,
chronobiologically and chronosociologically underpinned,
which range from the structuring of shift-work to the
reduction of jet lag; it seeks to be able to give practical
advice, in order to establish a new complementarity between change and continuity. It argues for the creation of
new periods of time in which vicissitudes can occur,

> events which – whether desirable or not – restore to life that
> dimension (of occurrence) that would then allow us to per-
> ceive and accept its discontinuities, its wrinkles, curves and
> cracks, and to be prepared for and to celebrate its beginning
> and its end. 'Vicissitudes' are to be a cipher for a life released
> from the coordinate system of 'work' and 'free time', a life
> good for something other than keeping the great machine
> functioning and one's own self fit for it. For what? . . . The
> question arises as to whether an appropriation of a more
> elementary kind would not have to occur before (or on,
> during) the politicization of a piece of 'new' time wrested
> from work and its correlate, free time: a conversion of work,
> free time, or rather freed time into living time, an opening up
> of the horizon of time to the unforeseen, which would be
> subjectively assimilable, manageable, and also: welcome.[12]

The third uchronia has a lot in store for women, since
they bring the better prerequisites for it with them. Men
are 'blind to the temporal quality of change' and hence all
the more at risk 'as far as the secret predominance of
vicissitudes which have been pushed aside is concerned
. . . as long as they (men) are functioning, they do not
notice that there is something the matter with them . . .
until . . . a . . . vicissitude notices them'. But in case

women and the women's movement should not summon up enough strength to switch off for men the conveyor belt on which they are processing their lives, perhaps the (even though only just germinating) longing for an 'alternative' experience of time, for a day 'from which one cannot already tell its evening in the morning, will suffice for this'.[13] 'All days are not equal', runs an inscription which Michael Young saw in Ghana. Did Africans realize the rediscovered Western uchronia long ago?

Uchronias, like utopias before them, have a central social function to fulfil: they contain proposed solutions to particular unsolved problems in a society. 'Utopias?', asks Hans Magnus Enzensberger, 'we cannot see them. We only feel them like a knife in our backs.' And it is strange how familiar the knives in our backs feel, as if they had been sticking there for a long time. The first knife is sharpened on the unsolved problems of an insatiable economy of time. After it has proved possible to produce more in less time, it is now a question of doing more, fitting in more work and leisure activities in potentially less time. The increase in productivity results in an increase in consumption – more consumer goods, leisure activities and journeys, more entertainment, communication and information contend for spans of attention and time to expend. Production presses for destruction, and rituals of destruction can be arranged in diverse ways, preformed by the archaic figure of the sacrifice. Consumption is a harmless form of destruction in comparison, even though the mountains of refuse are piling up. The uchronia which only demands more time does not escape the quantitative logic of money and its accumulation. Money and time remain substitutable, but the general money preference will predominate even when more time is demanded. More can also be got out of living time and more can be made of life. 'Squeeze out the 150%', they say in the USA. It will soon be more. Self-exploitation or drug? Both interpretations are permissible, but the knife turns in the back and hurts.[14] The uchronia of temporal autonomy is at least as old as the oppression of the workers who were crushed under the temporal regime of the machine age.[15] Paul Lafargue called his uchronically satirical ideas the right to laziness. But laziness as a vice and as a virtue has long since disappeared, comparable with that extinct sensation which was once called accidie. It overcame hermits in the form of the demon of midday heat, who sought to deter them from their duties of prayer.[16] The strict temporal discipline of Saint Benedict prevailed, though. Prayer was secularized, and work remained. The modern forms of this uchronia are more diverse. And it is all too understandable that the dream of freedom and self-determination is being dreamed anew in the face of a technological development which seems to make freedoms and new forms of decentralization possible in spatial and temporal terms. It is the expression of the struggle for political structuring, in which one part still remains attached to the quantitative logic of a reduction in working hours while constantly sticking to the status quo of rights secured, whereas another part is confronted with the almost insoluble problems of abolishing the rigid dividing lines between categories of favoured and disadvantaged workers, and striving for radically different patterns of distribution for all, including the possibility of a 'four-fifths working life'. It is a knife sticking in the backs of many people, and which a good many hands and many interests are helping to hone. But the prospects of organizations learning are contradictory. On the one hand, the collective knowledge of organizations is always selective and limited to what they have – successfully – learnt so far. On the other hand, organizations cannot do anything but 'relearn' if they want to survive in the face of changed environmental conditions. Even if the knowledge and the goals of individuals may be irrelevant to the store of knowledge and the objectives of an organization, the 'dissenting' views of its members can nevertheless become a

question of survival for an organization, when the legit-
imacy of the basis of its subsistence is affected by them:[17]
meanwhile the knife remains sticking in many people's
backs.

The third uchronia seeks to be culturally innovative. It
returns to the biological and cultural heritage, suppressed
in the machine age, which, newly authenticated in scientific terms, tries to combine preservation and mutation,
change and continuity in optimal fashion. It has an
appellative air, and starts, like the other uchronias, from
individual everyday experience. If only enough people
begin to change their lives – the great doctrines of humanity commenced in this manner. But how do long-
established time systems of institutions, determined by
specific interests, change? Cannot enough examples of
planned 'spontaneity' be cited, which is already inherent
in the design of the system, or of 'vicissitudes' which can
give the illusion, with clever statistical methods, that they
have been brought about by 'chance' or the individual?
One can also yield to the pressure for social justice in
queues of waiting people by installing a generator of
chance, or – as happened at an American airport because
of complaints by passengers who had to wait too long
for their luggage – the plane can be parked in a remote
spot to prolong the journey time of passengers to the
arrivals lounge, but to reduce the waiting period for
their luggage.[18] Experts call this awareness management.
Numerous studies are commissioned whose goal consists
solely in finding out how time which people spend waiting
can be more entertainingly, more 'spontaneously', and
also economically better used. Not just in the former
USSR, but also in the USA people spend on average thirty
minutes a day waiting in a queue, which makes a total of
thirty-seven thousand million hours a year: a hitherto
unused potential for the marketing of further products and
of services.

It is easy to see that even the culturally innovative uchronic time-strategies, which in their fine structure may be coordinated with the latest findings on the biological rhythms of human beings, their social preferences and their desires for social justice or sociability, cannot escape the danger of manipulation, indeed of perversion. Thus the third knife is also sticking deep in the back of this society. Is time pressing to remove the knives? Who are the victims, and whose victims are they?

However different the three current uchronias, the economic, the political and the cultural one, may be in their initial position, however differently they may judge the causes and describe the solutions to be adopted, however collective or individual the prescribed strategies of action may look – they have one thing in common: time is mainly experienced as an externalized constraint, influencing people from outside, which it is necessary to counteract. The constraint can be impersonal or personalized, can appear in the form of employers, of society or as an -ism, but it confronts people as something given, something made by others. Time here appears in the mask, the most neutral image of which is the clock. It is a mask which threatens, denies wishes, suppresses and expropriates them. It is the mask of time which causes suffering and which has inevitable death in store in the end. For even in the boldest uchronias, one liberation is not conceivable: the liberation from the temporal limitations of the existence of every individual human life.

Sartre related the following about his friend Paul Nizan and his disappointed expectations on a trip to the Soviet Union: 'he went to Russia because he wanted to find out whether people were now no longer afraid of death after the revolution, whether death had become something of secondary importance for them.' Then Nizan had gone there and had seen that the Russians thought of death in the same way as we do, and as a result had come back disappointed. He had said at the time – in an unmistakable tone of resignation – to Sartre: 'On this point, no, there's nothing to be done, they haven't changed.'[19]

In view of the final truth, that of one's own death, all human beings are victims of time. The mask of the constraint which seems to emanate from time is nothing other than protection from this truth. In this respect, we cannot take it off completely, but it ought to be possible to look behind it a bit more. For the victims merrily carry on acting in the meantime.

Time is made by human beings and has to do with power which they exercise over one another with the aid of strategies of time. Time unites and separates – combatants as well as lovers. As with every form of power, there is a counter-power; every strategy finds its counter-strategy. Time is in everything, as Shinmen Musashi, a famous Japanese warrior, sums up the strategies of his art of war (*Go Rin No Sho*) in 1645: time is important in dancing and in music, since rhythms exist only when the time is right. But there is also time in all skills, and equally in the void. Time determines the life of the warrior, his rise and decline, his harmonies and discords. In order to be able to think and act strategically, one has to know which time is to be used, and when it is not to be used . . . from the small to the big, from the fast to the slow, from the time of the distance to the time of the background. Without knowing the time of the background, every strategy becomes uncertain in its outcome. It is a book, incidentally, which became almost compulsory reading for American managers in view of the challenge of Japanese economic power.[20]

The strategic use of time as a central aspect in the emergence of power, and for the purpose of maintaining it, runs throughout the whole of social life, from interpersonal relations to the big institutions and their built-in tendencies to persist. It begins with the child, who always places the state of consciousness he or she has just experienced at the centre of the perception of time, and in whom immediacy follows immediacy. From the periodicity of the body, he or she develops the first ideas of time, but also the first strategies in dealing with time. In the rhythm of breathing, eating and sleeping, the child experiences his or her earliest gratifications and privations. With the control of the sphincter muscles, the child develops a little later the most important instrument for implementing its independent consciousness of time, with the aid of which it becomes possible to make adults, all-powerful up to that time, dependent on its own will in a way. But society and outside determination already intervene here. The pleasure contained in the independent scanning of its bodily functions makes it terribly hard for the child, under the pressure of its surroundings, to give up its original perception of time. Alienness abstracts from all pleasure.[21] In a fine essay, Caroline Neubaur has studied the experiences and theoretical insights of the English psychiatrist Donald W. Winnicott. Precisely in the early mother–child relationship, a situation is produced which is characterized by alienation. There are illusions which thwart one another and which consist in the fact that two 'interior' systems confront one another which have usurped the other's 'exterior' in each case, but which cannot perceive one another as illusory. So that the alienation can be removed, something has to be added which is perceptible to both sides, which has an element of estrangement for both, and yet is capable of removing estrangement. According to Winnicott, this third element is the transitional object which can be accepted by both sides as something alien. For this it is necessary that an effort has to be made on the part of the child as well as on the part of the mother: namely to accept a bit of alienness in order to be able to overcome alienness.[22]

Paradoxically, it could be continued, proper time is made possible only through the time of others. Only when a common time is created as a frame of reference, which neither belongs completely to the one or completely to the other nor is occupied by him or her, can the constraint of time at least be loosened, even if it cannot be totally removed. Between two individuals, this presupposes a process of constant development, of negotiation and argument by means of their continued temporal strategies. Many sets of strategies are at the disposal of strategic action in time and through time: accelerating or slowing down; fixing a deadline; promising; waiting and keeping the other waiting; acting at the right moment, deciding or biding one's time. What links these social situations with one another, which recur in countless variants and in which people fix time symbolically, but with real consequences, is the interval. Just like Winnicott's transitional object, the teddy bear or the corner of a cushion which slips between mother and child and becomes a powerful means of symbolizing experience and gaining reality that becomes fundamental to human creativity per se, the interval of time is the basic element for structuring interhuman relations. Waiting and keeping the other waiting, promising, deciding, fixing a deadline – in countless variations and combinations, fighting or loving relationships can be shaped by these. Abolishing the interval would mean abolishing strategy.[23] The interval can be consciously and intentionally used; it can result from situations of social inequality or be the expression of power and consolidate the latter. The brilliantly strategic approach to time manifests itself in the interval.

But the interval is never fixed once and for all, it flows with time and remains, like power and status, renegotiable. In the case of keeping someone waiting, to cite the example of one of the most ordinary and most banal situations, the time of others is disposed of by their time remaining unoccupied. Language has no expression for the person who keeps someone waiting, but only for the person waiting. Yet even the obvious powerlessness of the person waiting, in which differentials of power and status are expressed, is limited and open to counter-strategies.

Promises, on the other hand, extend the interval for a certain or uncertain time. Promises presuppose trust, and trust saves time, but promises are conditionally open to the demand that they are kept and are consequently also subject to the strategy of the interval. Fixing a deadline, on the other hand, sets limits; the interval is given a time-limit and sanctioned; it is tested as an instrument of power, but even deadlines are negotiable.

The interval structures interhuman relations, by the flow of time being indicated, interrupted, slowed down, accelerated, restricted or given a time-limit. From this it becomes clear that it is part of the peculiarity of the concept of time to be not just a symbol of a widespread synthesis, of an abstraction at a high level, but a symbol of the changing relations between individuals.[24] It also becomes understandable that certain social conditions are required in which decisions in a temporal context become possible in the first place. In situations in which time is socially negated, because the situation is not one oriented towards continuation or termination in which the socially expected duration is negated, there is no interval and no decision. '"Choice" would indeed have no meaning if it did not constitute a discontinuity or a non-determined selection, but it would be equally meaningless if this selection had no consequences, i.e. did not result in a sequel or constituted a sequence.'[25] The strategic game with the interval, the fixing of time as a structuring of relations, is based on the search for the right moment. Everybody thinks they know it, or longs for it. It holds good equally for individuals and for organizations, indeed even for nations. Firms have to decide whether and when they should expand or diversify; when they should buy or sell on the market; political parties have to decide on the right moment to call new elections or not. These are the moments which make history or which can at least be reconstructed in retrospect as turning points in history. The losers, asserts Koselleck, have been the better historians over thousands of years because their primary experience, unlike that of the victors, is above all that everything has turned out differently from what was planned or hoped for. They have, if they reflect methodically, to produce more evidence to explain why something has turned out differently.[26] But if the right moment proves to be such only in retrospect, it is the interval which makes it possible in the first place.

The interval, once it is transported from the level of interhuman relations into the time-structure of institutions, changes its quality there. Of course, as a strategic instrument of power it remains effective there too. The priority of the fixed deadline within bureaucratic organizations is an example which has already been cited; establishing temporal priorities is a means of reducing complexity. But while people, who confront others as beings who confer meaning, symbolically interact, and communicate with one another, even though antagonistically, fix time by inventing intervals, playing with them, and 'making' time themselves in the succession of interhuman actions, in ritual gestures and customs, in skilful delaying tactics, in promising or running up debts, the time of institutions faces them as something more viscous, already made, if not even frozen. The frequent use of the term 'time', as if time possessed an independent existence, is connected not least with the fact that time in social facilities and institutions becomes relatively independent of individuals. Just as the means of determining time, whether created by human beings or not, have a motion of their own, since it is a question of socially standardized motions which have a certain degree of independence from other motions and from other human and non-human changes, the individual person has to coordinate his or her own behaviour with the established time of the group to which he or she belongs, and with the organizations which surround him or her.

It is this alienation of time, occurring through its concentration within institutions, which then reacts as something external, is felt to be a constraint, and can be used as an instrument of power. Where the interval in the interhuman sphere is relatively open and can be shaped, it becomes rigid where it is a question of legally regulated deadlines on which sanctions are imposed; where the credit apparatus sets deadlines and makes money work; where it is a matter of waiting periods which are fixed, tolerated and dictated by organizations and within them. A broad field of activity presents itself here for intercultural and interorganizational comparison: who has to wait, how long, what for and how, can serve as an indicator of the value which time – whose time? – is given within an organization. But in this way the original conditions for the slow consolidation of the interval, its embedding in power structures, can also be understood.

Power, exercised by central authorities, establishes itself over space and over time. Territorially established rule was followed by the temporal kind. The early big empires used both forms to consolidate their rule, but first it was more urgent to control the space, the territory. There were spatial strategies for this – the exercise of physical force, and taxation – and incipient temporal ones, which particularly included the introduction of writing and written documents by the bureaucracies.[27] For now it could be established what was and ought to be the case. The temporal aspect of the exercise of power is openly revealed in dictatorships even today. Regimes founded on terror also use temporal strategies. Terror is exercised through the unforeseeability, the temporal arbitrariness, with which victims are taken away and turned into victims. In military dictatorships, moreover, Montesquieu's separation of powers between executive, legislature and judiciary is abolished by denying their temporal connections. For jurisdiction stands for what happened in the past. The past is judged, and decisions are made about right and wrong in retrospect. The legislature, however, points to the future. Laws are made in order to establish norms of behaviour and situations which are only those set. The executive, however, executes sheer present; it establishes and determines what is, and has to prevail, now. In military dictatorships, past and future are simultaneously denied with the abolition of an independent jurisdiction and an independent parliament. All power is granted to the executive, which alone has to determine what has to prevail in the present that rules over the other times.[28]

In the development of societies, the territorial rule which was exercised by means of the spatial concept of 'order' is followed by that which has devoted itself to the dynamized concept of motion, 'progress', progress through acceleration. Acceleration uses time as motion for strategic goals. Deadly in battle, quickness, i.e. being quicker than the others, has been preserved in competition and is being cultivated in increasingly sophisticated form. Economic competition, now spread throughout the world and functioning as a driving force of world economic events, remains ultimately rooted in that development which uses the acceleration of the machine to increase productivity. Laboratory time, which is inherent in the new communication technologies, is employed to economic advantage to transfer information to other areas of production and of services, to create additional infrastructures, and for the purpose of continued accelerated scientific and technological innovation. Acceleration facilitates mobility, and mobility promises further mobilization. Even sport, the institutionalized competition of bodies in aggressive conflicts, prepared in a way suited to the media, between nations and regions, towns and districts, ultimately appears as an appendage to the extra-somatically accelerated body-machine. In the struggle for, and the cult surrounding, the proverbial tenths of a second, scientifically based training methods are used which are able to take into account the bodily functions of athletes dependent on their biorhythms, as well as the smallest advantages which technological equipment has to offer. A gigantic machinery of innovation has been set in motion here, which leads to a powerfully growing branch of industry ranging from the solitary sport of body-building to the frenzied stages of experimentation by industry in motor racing. In view of this collective cult of speed, from which no nation is exempt, the strategies of slowing down look really pathetic and defensive: cycleways are set up in the towns, speed limits introduced on the motorways, and for his novel *The Discovery of Slowness* the author Sten Nadolny needed a historical figure who, in his strange habits of thought and perception, seemed eerie even to his contemporaries. The braking experiments will undoubtedly be continued and in part even institutionalized – but is not a well-functioning braking device part of every decently constructed machine? Must not everyone who operates a machine know in what circumstances it is to be accelerated and in what circumstances it is to be slowed down? Thus slowness is ultimately cancelled out in the continued acceleration; the latter relativizes itself through the former. Social development does not proceed totally in conformity with machines, of course, but the interdependences are irreversibly aimed at acceleration. The Stone Age reflex of quickness in flight and in battle has developed throughout social evolution into a scientific and technological civilization which is continuing to accelerate. This is the time of the background which it is of central importance for every other temporal strategy to recognize.

Sociologists and anthropologists long ago referred to the symbolic, time-setting and structuring process by means of which 'social time' is created by human beings and between them. For Norbert Elias, a glance back at Galileo's experiments shows *in vivo*, as it were, the departure of the concept of time in physics from the matrix of social time centred on human beings, which was linked with a corresponding change in the concept of nature.[29] For him, the division into a time of physics and a social time is closely connected with the rise of physics and the natural sciences in general, which led to a conceptual dualism. In this respect, scientists have superseded priests in establishing the 'right' moment which signifies rise or decline and is the decisive factor for chaos and order, no matter whether it is derived from the detected correspondence with the happenings of the gods or from the scientifically based investigation of nature and its processes. Elias gives a detailed account of the contents of the novel by an African author, Chinua Achebe, which focuses on a conflict over determining time. It concerns a first-hand report of life in an Ibo village in Eastern Nigeria during the period in which the old way of life was just beginning to change under the influence of colonial power. The focal point of the novel is the high priest who serves the god of six villages, and one of whose most important functions is to proclaim the right moment. It was indicated by the arrival of the new moon, for which the priest had to be on the look-out and which was to be greeted as a welcome guest. People's business was dependent on the arrival of the new moon, as well as the festivals and the beginning of harvest time with which the New Year was inaugurated. Achebe/Elias sympathetically describe what it meant for people to learn the right moment from an authority integrating their activities, and the way in which knowledge of the secrets of determining time represented a source of the priest's power. They give insight into an early form of the experience of time and demonstrate how important it was for people to hear the proclamation that the time for the harvest had come. For when, after a dramatic worsening of the conflict with the colonial administration, the priest falls silent and does not proclaim harvest time, people begin to starve.

But what does the right moment stand for, and what can it be measured against? The longing for the individual moment can be strategically directed outwards, in order pragmatically to seek knowledge of the 'when' which can be translated into real advantages. It can be the planned or

the chance moment, but it is always a question of relating
it to human action. Knowing the right moment is useful;
determining it confers power and promises control. But
the search for the moment can also point inwards, to the
unfolding of one's own, temporal self, to the development
of an identity repeatedly reassembled from fragments.
Then time is made by the flow of time momentarily stopping to let in the unexpected, to break routine, and to be
open to the experience of spontaneity and to the 'vicissitudes' of life. Like the playfully and culturally creative
transitional space in which the child discovers the transitional object and creates it himself or herself at the same
time, a 'time of transition' is discovered and created here.
Through the unreal suspension, the momentary standstill
of a present withdrawn from duration, the time of transition also contributes to the paradox of the real–unreal:
for the real becomes real only in a process of reduction and
elimination of the possible.[30] In the long run, the moment
is not stoppable, it flows back into the continuum of time.
But this moment contains the power which can turn the
transition itself into development. The poetic language of
Cacciari, who follows great Hebrew, Christian and Islamic
scholasticism, speaks of the *nunc instantis*, the dimension
of a temporary interim period, which in its fullness is so
temporary, but also so present, that it can hardly be
noticed as an instant of time and yet for this very reason is
completely transitory – a dimension of total transitoriness,
in which the most temporary instant coincides with the
moment that remains and that blows open the continuum.
At this moment, which interrupts the flowing of instants,
it is possible 'to take to heart' the sparks of hope, and 'to
brush history the wrong way'; at this moment it is possible
to understand 'how the radical imperfection of the world
. . . is not mere despair on account of the ruins, but is the
power which can raise those sparks in things in all their
transitoriness. There is the temporary interim period of a
Yes which is stronger than catastrophe, that But which

unmasks the idolatry of the homogeneous and empty continuum.'[31]

But like knowledge that can be a game, playing with the moment also follows rules which lead from the sphere of the unreal into that of reality. For Winnicott, children discover and invent reality while playing; they play so that they can surprise themselves. In the game, the child discovers the self, which stands separately and differently, but in relation to the reality which it is not. Even for playing, it is central to set, shift and learn to keep to limits. Only because what 'prevails' constantly shifts is insight possible.

Separation from the mother occurs via a space, the transitional space, and with the aid of transitional objects which belong neither to internal psychological reality nor to the external one. The game has the constructive function of creating this space, which stimulates the creative abilities of the child. Winnicott develops a theory of culture as a continuation of the idea of the transitional object. The game of the child who finds an object whose creator he or she is 'in reality', and its continuation in the cultural creativity of the adult, take place in a space situated between the external world and internal psychological reality. For Winnicott, the 'intermediate realm is the actual source of power for that which sets inside and outside in motion. Plunging into the intermediate realm means being able to intervene in the outside world with new energy.'[32] But all this also takes place in the interim period. Creativity, the creative production of culture, requires not just space, but also time. The child has to learn to rid himself or herself of the initial illusion of his or her omnipotence so that he or she can create new illusions as an adult, in the transitional space and in the transitional time between the real and the unreal, which is not yet real. The game and its continuation as a cultural creative achievement is a great loosening-up exercise, creating subjects anew – an achievement which breaks rules and cancels systems, and thus gives the person playing the possibility of becoming a creator of culture himself or herself a little, through fruitful chaos.

Playing time games, shifting limits, trying out 'what prevails' and setting new limits is, as shown above, an essential part of the symbolic power of action between individuals. But the search for the moment goes on, not least in the sciences. Knowledge of the strategic moment seems imperative for practical application, and even Nietzsche suspected that fear of the unpredictable was the ulterior instinct of science. But the search for the moment can be interpreted in another sense: as an inquiry into the first moment, the origin, in which the universe could have arisen and time along with it. The time of physics, which with the advance of the natural sciences separated from the matrix of social time and which in the machine age became the ideologically linear guide rail for progress, to which all other time had to submit in the name of its external, objective reality, is beginning to approach the social conception of time again. Not just because the intensified study of the possible origins of the universe, and particularly of the question whether it was a unique event from the point of view of physics, can be interpreted as a kind of time game on the part of physicists. Prigogine and Stengers speak of a new coherence which is beginning to emerge between different scientific disciplines, and which is beginning to open up to the 'problem of development' in general. The concept of the 'event', for instance, has changed in that it is now the event which accounts for the difference between past and future, whereas wherever the arrow of time is denied in physics, past and future are regarded as equivalent.[33] What physics has recently discovered is that most, if not all, cyclical phenomena can be 'chaotic' and vice versa. Transitions between the time of 'unreproducible' and the time of 'reproducible' phenomena thus become possible in both directions. For the time of reproducible phenomena, we can therefore speak of a reversal of time, since the flow of events can be reversed, i.e. without the observed events changing the development already completed can be retraced. For chaotic phenomena, however, it is not possible to reconstruct their past or to reproduce them. Accordingly, there would also be two kinds of evolution.

At the moment, it is not yet certain whether the explosive phenomena which could have occurred with the big bang belong to the sphere of 'reproducible' or 'unreproducible' time. Prigogine and Stengers suspect that the hypothesis of the uniqueness of the cosmological beginning, according to which there must have been a 'zero time', is to be abandoned. They suggest instead that the universe could have arisen, in a kind of 'gratuitous action', from fluctuations of the vacuum, from the motions of mass and energy which together amount to zero. In the beginning, there would therefore have been no unique event, but a transition between states of entropy stemming from a fluctuation – a fluctuation not unlike that between chaos and order.

Recently, another physicist, Stephen W. Hawking, has likewise suggested abandoning the hypothesis of the uniqueness of the big bang. Uniqueness would be the state in which the space-time continuum has shrunk to an infinitely dense, infinitely small point, a state which cannot be described in terms of physics and in which time has no significance. Among other things, he tries to answer the question why at least three arrows of time point from the past into the future, even though the laws of physics do not distinguish between the directions pointing forwards and those pointing backwards: the thermodynamic arrow of time, according to which disorder is increasing; the psychological arrow of time, according to which the past but not the future remains in the memory; and the cosmological arrow, according to which the universe is expanding and not shrinking. Hawking now hopes that a new, yet to be discovered, great, uniform theory (quantum gravitation) could lead to the conclusion that the space-time continuum does not represent a 'line' which begins with the big bang and ends with the great collapse, but is a 'loop' without beginning and end. According to his proposal, the space-time continuum would admittedly be boundless, but not infinite, just as the earth appears boundless to a stroller, even though it is finitely vast. But human beings, and hence knowledge of the universe and time, could only exist in the expanding phase. They represent a tiny fraction of order within an increasingly disorderly universe[34] – enough, however, to lead the social matrix back into nature.

What do such 'time games' on the part of the natural scientists mean for people today, for their desire for proper time, and for their longings to escape the constraint of time and to be able to structure time differently? How can the complex balancing acts in the daily juxtaposition of times be better accomplished, and how will a society within the extended present cope with the current problems of accelerated innovation, increasing routine, and throwing away? Having time to play with the moment, being able to plunge into the interim period of transitions, presupposes a recognition of how this time is constituted and how it can be created. The 'this way and no other' which scientific knowledge has to offer includes the 'now this way' and 'now the other' as a possibility of being able to intervene and structure things, at least under certain conditions. The glance behind the mask in which time appears in social life makes it possible to stage the game differently as well, starting from a changed sense of time which, like every feeling, is itself the result of history, of experience.

Cronos's fear which caused him to consume his stock, his children, has not been able to hold back the new age with its activities spewing forth innovations. With machines, other motions and speeds entered social life and changed people's perceptive faculty. An even more accelerated, yet more diffuse quality of time, because pressing for constant availability, adheres to today's machines. Machines and people are forming new temporal combinations, just as the relations between people, mediated with one another via machines, are assuming a different shape. The social arrow of time also points forwards. The constraints which seem to emanate from time have not been broken, but the game, the team-game, may perhaps be loosening up. The longing for proper time has become publicly communicable, but proper time is made possible only by others. It is up to the children of Cronos to seize the moment which presents itself to them from so many sides. It is not a question of the unique first moment, but of the socially perceptible one. It is necessary to discover and to shape it – as a repeatable moment which fluctuates to and fro between social chaos and social order, between the self of proper time and the time of society.

It will then become apparent whether the children of Cronos have emancipated themselves.

Postscript

What reflection concerning the irregular sequence of dates 1884, 1885, 1886, 1888, 1892, 1893, 1904 did Bloom make before their arrival at their destination?

He reflected that the progressive extension of the field of individual development and experience was regressively accompanied by a restriction of the converse domain of interindividual relations.

As in what ways?

From inexistence to existence he came to many and was as one received: existence with existence he was with any as any with any: from existence to nonexistence gone he would be by all as none perceived.

James Joyce, Ulysses

Notes

The literature of social science on the subject of time is extremely extensive. For a systematic review see Helga Nowotny, *Time and Social Theory. Towards a Social Theory of Time: Time & Society*, 1992 Sage (London, Newbury Park and New Delhi), vol. 1 (3), 421–54. The following notes do not therefore aim to be a bibliographical guide. They contain merely the references given in connection with the text, and a few further ones.

Introduction

1 Ilya Prigogine and Isabelle Stengers, *Entre le Temps et l'Eternité*, Paris: Fayard, 1988.
2 Helga Nowotny, 'Time Structuring and Time Measurement: On the Interrelation Between Timekeepers and Social Time', in: J. T. Fraser and N. Lawrence (eds), *The Study of Time II*, Berlin and Heidelberg: Springer Verlag, 1975.
3 See among others Paola Reale, *Tempo e Identità*, Milan: F. Angeli, 1988; Uwe Arnold and Peter Heintel (eds), *Zeit und Identität*, Vienna: Verlag des Verbandes der wissenschaftlichen Gesellschaften Österreichs, 1983; Friedrich Fürstenberg and Ingo Mörth (eds), *Zeit als*

Strukturelement von Lebenswelt und Gesellschaft, Linz: Universitätsverlag R. Trauner, 1986.

Chapter 1 The Illusion of Simultaneity

1 Adolf Holl, *Der letzte Christ*, Stuttgart: Deutsche Verlagsanstalt, 1979, p. 9.
2 Norman F. Ramsey, 'Precise Measurement of Time', *American Scientist*, vol. 76, 42–9.
3 Stephen Kern, *The Culture of Time and Space 1880–1918*, Cambridge, Mass.: Harvard University Press, 1983.
4 Ernst Mach, *Die Mechanik in ihrer Entwicklung historisch-kritisch dargestellt*, Leipzig, 1883.
5 See Kern, *Culture of Time and Space*, pp. 19, 25.
6 Ilya Prigogine and Isabelle Stengers, *Entre le Temps et l'Eternité*, Paris: Fayard, 1988.
7 William James, 'On Some Omissions of Introspective Psychology', *Mind*, Jan. 1884; as well as *Principles of Psychology*, New York, 1890.
8 H. Hubert and M. Mauss, 'Etude sommaire de la représentation du temps dans la religion et la magie', in: *Melanges d'histoire des religions*, Paris, 1909, quoted from Kern, *Culture of Time and Space*, p. 32.
9 Eviatar Zerubavel, 'The Standardization of Time: A Sociohistorical Perspective', *American Journal of Sociology*, vol. 88, 1–23.
10 Kern, *Culture of Time and Space*.
11 Ibid.
12 Office of Technology Assessment, *Technology and the American Economic Transition*, Washington, D.C., 1988.
13 Alexander Szalai, *The Uses of Time*, The Hague: Mouton, 1972.
14 Thomas P. Hughes, *Networks of Power: Electrification in Western Society, 1880–1930*, Baltimore: John Hopkins University Press, 1983.
15 Sten Nadolny, *Die Entdeckung der Langsamkeit*, Munich: Piper, 1983, pp. 208–9.
16 Enno Neumann, 'Arbeitslos – Zeitlos', in: Rainer Zoll

(ed.), *Zerstörung und Wiederaneignung von Zeit*, Frankfurt: Suhrkamp, 1988, pp. 267–75.

17   Credit and debt produce a complex relationship of temporal dependence between debtors and creditors, to which too little attention has been paid by the social sciences up to now.

18   Johannes Fabian, *Time and the Other: How Anthropology Makes its Object*, New York: Columbia University Press, 1983.

19   Jean-Jacques Salomon and Andre Lebeau, *L'écrivain public et l'ordinateur. Mirages du développement*, Paris: Hachette, 1988.

20   Norbert Elias, *Die Gesellschaft der Individuen*, Frankfurt: Suhrkamp, 1987; English translation *The Society of Individuals*, Oxford: Blackwell, 1991.

21   Marie Jahoda, Paul F. Lazarsfeld and Hans Zeisel, *Die Arbeitslosen von Marienthal*, 2nd edn, Allensbach: Verlag für Demoskopie, 1960; Marie Jahoda, *Employment and Unemployment*, Cambridge University Press, 1982.

22   J. Le Goff, 'Zeit der Kirche und Zeit des Händlers im Mittelalter', in: Claudia Honegger (ed.), *Schrift und Materie in der Geschichte. Vorschläge zur systematischen Aneignung historischer Prozesse*, Frankfurt, 1977, pp. 393–414; R. Wendorff, *Zeit und Kultur-Geschichte des Zeitbewußtseins in Europa*, Opladen: Westdeutscher Verlag, 1980.

23   J. Goody and I. Watt, 'The Consequences of Literacy', *Comparative Studies in Society and History*, vol. 5 (1962–3), 304–26, 332–45.

24   Sherry Turkle, 'The Subjective Computer: Study in the Psychology of Personal Computing', *Social Studies of Science*, vol. 12, 2 (1982), 173–205.

25   Magoroh Maruyama, 'The New Logic of Japan's Young Generation', *Technological Forecasting and Social Change*, vol. 28 (1985), 351–64.

26   Michael Young, *The Metronomic Society: Natural Rhythms and Human Timetables*, London: Thames and Hudson, 1988, p. 163.

27   Niklas Luhmann, *Archimedes und wir*, Berlin: Merve Verlag, 1987.

28 Reinhart Koselleck, 'Erfahrungswandel und Methoden-wechsel: Eine historisch-anthropologische Skizze', in: *Theorie der Geschichte*, 1988, p. 48.

Chapter 2 From the Future to the Extended Present

1 Hans Blumenberg, *Lebenszeit und Weltzeit*, Frankfurt: Suhrkamp, 1986, p. 223.
2 Ibid., p. 225.
3 Ibid., pp. 239–40.
4 Ibid., p. 242.
5 An increase in productivity due to technological im-provements can be traced in Western political economies from roughly 1880 on. Nathan Rosenberg, *Perspectives on Technology*, Cambridge: Cambridge University Press, 1976.
6 The classic essay on this is that by E. P. Thompson, 'Time, Work-discipline and Industrial Capitalism', *Past and Present*, vol. 38 (December 1967), 56–97.
7 Reinhart Koselleck, *Vergangene Zukunft: Zur Semantik geschichtlicher Zeiten*, Frankfurt: Suhrkamp, 1979.
8 W. C. Clark and R. E. Munn (eds), *Sustainable Develop-ment of the Biosphere*, Cambridge: Cambridge University Press, 1986.
9 A good survey of recent studies in the area of time and organization is given by Allen C. Bluedorn and Robert B. Dernhardt, 'Time and Organization', *Journal of Management*, vol. 14, no. 2 (1988), 299–320.
10 G. H. von Wright, *Time, Chance and Contradiction*, Cam-bridge: Cambridge University Press, 1968.
11 A more detailed account of this can be found in Helga Nowotny, 'From the Future to the Extended Present: Time in Social Systems', in: G. Kirsch et al. (eds), *The Formu-lation of Time Preferences in a Multidisciplinary Perspective*, Aldershot: Gower, 1988, pp. 17–31.
12 Mark Elchardus, 'The Rediscovery of Chronos: The New Role of Time in Sociological Theory', *International So-ciology*, vol. 3, no. 1 (March 1988), 35–60, also comes to

the following conclusion from a different theoretical perspective:

> One consequence of the shift from history in natural sui generis time to the temporality of systems is that the future can no longer be taken for granted. This disappearance of the future has nothing to do with pessimism. It is a consequence of the greater awareness of the fact that social systems create their own time and that the idea of a future is only meaningful to the extent the present and the future can be linked through some (relative) invariance and some sequence.

13 R. Nelson and S. G. Winter, 'In Search of a Useful Theory of Innovation', *Research Policy*, vol. 6 (1977), 36–76; Brian Arthur, 'Competing Technologies: An Overview', in: G. Dosi et al. (eds), *Technical Chance and Economic Theory*, London: F. Pinter, 1988.

14 Numerous halls are already fully booked up for New Year's Eve parties to see in the year 2000. *Der Spiegel*, no. 1, 1988.

15 Norbert Elias, *Über die Zeit*, Frankfurt: Suhrkamp, 1984; English translation *Time: An Essay*, Oxford: Blackwell, 1992.

16 Florence R. Kluckhohn and Fred L. Strodtbeck (eds), *Variations in Value Orientations*, Evanston, Ill.: Row & Peterson, 1962.

17 Krzysztof Pomian, *L'ordre du temps*, Paris: Editions Gallimard, 1984.

18 Michael Young, *The Metronomic Society: Natural Rhythms and Human Timetables*, London: Thames and Hudson, 1988.

19 The classic works on this are Lewis Mumford, *Technics and Civilization*, New York: Harcourt, 1934; and David Landes, *Revolution in Time*, Cambridge, Mass.: Harvard University Press, 1983.

20 Elias, *Über die Zeit*.

21 Siegfried Kracauer, 'Ahasverus, or the Riddle of Time', in: *History, The Last Things Before The Last*, New York: Oxford University Press, 1969.

22 Lars Clausen, 'Prognose und Epignose', *Österreichische Zeitschrift für Soziologie*, vol. 12, no. 4 (1987), 21–9; Gerhard Schmied, *Soziale Zeit, Umfang, Geschwindigkeit und Evolution*, Berlin: Duncker & Humblot, 1985.

23 Anthony Giddens, *The Constitution of Society: Outline of the Theory of Structuration*, Cambridge: Polity Press, 1984.

24 Young, *Metronomic Society*.

25 For a survey see Joshua A. Goldstein, *Long Cycles*, New Haven and London: Yale University Press, 1988; for the social sciences see Renate Mayntz, *Soziale Diskontinuitäten: Erscheinungsformen und Ursachen*, Cologne: Max Planck Institut für Gesellschaftsforschung, discussion paper 87/1.

26 Cesare Marchetti, 'Society as a Learning System: Discovery, Invention and Innovation Cycles Revisited', *Technological Forecasting and Social Change*, vol. 18 (1980), 267–82; 'The Future', Laxenburg: IIASA June 1986, mimeo.

27 See Horst Kern, *Empirische Sozialforschung*, Munich: C. H. Beck, 1982.

28 Robert U. Ayres, *The Next Industrial Revolution*, Cambridge: Ballinger, 1984; Mancur Olson, *The Rise and Fall of Nations*, New Haven, Conn.: Yale University Press, 1982.

29 André Leroi-Gourhan, *Geste et la parole*; German translation *Hand und Wort: Die Evolution von Sprache, Technik und Kunst*, Frankfurt: Suhrkamp, 1980, pp. 396–7.

30 Ibid., p. 397.

31 George Kubler, *The Shape of Time*, New Haven and London: Yale University Press, 1962.

32 Reinhart Koselleck, 'Fortschritt', in: *Geschichtliche Grundbegriffe: Historisches Lexikon zur politisch-sozialen Sprache in Deutschland*, Stuttgart 1979, p. 410.

Chapter 3 Cronos's Fear of the New Age

1 Bruno Latour and Steve Woolgar, *Laboratory Life: The Social Construction of Scientific Facts*, Beverley Hills: Sage Publications, 1979; Karin Knorr, *Die Fabrikation von Erkenntnis*, Frankfurt: Suhrkamp, 1981.

2 Bruno Latour, 'Les vues de l'Esprit', *Culture technique*, no. 14 (June 1985), 5–29.

3 Karin Knorr, 'Das naturwissenschaftliche Labor als Ort der "Verdichtung" von Gesellschaft', *Zeitschrift für Soziologie*, vol. 17, no. 2 (April 1988), 85–101.

4 Ibid.; Frank A. Dubinskas (ed.), *Making Time: Ethnographics of High-Technology Organizations*, Philadelphia: Temple University Press, 1988.

5 Hans Blumenberg, *Lebenszeit und Weltzeit*, Frankfurt: Suhrkamp, 1986, p. 236.

6 Martin Rudwick, *The Great Devonian Controversy: The Shaping of Scientific Knowledge among Gentlemanly Specialists*, Chicago: University of Chicago Press, 1985.

7 Stephen Jay Gould, 'A Triumph of Historical Excavation', *New York Review of Books*, 27 February 1986, 9–15.

8 Geoffrey Charles Bowker, 'If Time Ever Was: The Social and Scientific Perception of Time in England and France in the 1830s'. Unpublished Ph.D. dissertation, University of Melbourne, n.d.

9 Wolfgang Schivelbusch, *Geschichte der Eisenbahnreise: Zur Industrialisierung von Raum und Zeit im 19. Jahrhundert*, Munich: Carl Hanser Verlag, 1977.

10 Massimo Cacciari, *Zeit ohne Kronos*, Klagenfurt: Ritter Verlag, 1986, p. 23.

11 Reinhart Koselleck, 'Neuzeit. Zur Semantik moderner Bewegungsbegriffe', in: *Studien zum Beginn der modernen Welt*, Stuttgart: Klett-Cotta, 1977.

12 Blumenberg, *Lebenszeit und Weltzeit*, p. 226.

13 Rudolf Stichweh, 'Selbstorganisation in der Entstehung des modernen Wissenschaftssystems', mimeo; Michel Foucault, *Les Mots et les Choses*, Paris: Gallimard, 1966; English translation *The Order of Things*, London: Tavistock Publications, 1970.

14 Reinhart Koselleck, 'Fortschritt', in: *Geschichtliche Grundbegriffe: Historisches Lexikon zur politisch-sozialen Sprache in Deutschland*, Stuttgart, 1979, p. 393; Wolfgang Krohn, *Francis Bacon*, Munich: Beck, 1987.

15 Joseph Schumpeter, *Theorie der wirtschaftlichen Entwicklung*, 2nd edition, Munich–Leipzig, 1926; *Konjunkturzyklen: Eine theoretische, historische und statistische Analyse des kapitalistischen Prozesses*, vol. 1, Göttingen, 1951. See also Eduard März, *Joseph Alois Schumpeter – Forscher, Lehrer und Politiker*, Vienna: Verlag für Geschichte und Politik, 1983.

16 Giovanni Dosi, 'Technological Paradigms and Technological Trajectories', in: G. Dosi, C. Freeman, R. Nelson, G. Silverberg and L. Soete (eds), *Technical Change and Economic Theory*, London: Francis Pinter, 1988; R. Nelson and S. Winter, 'In Search of a Useful Theory of Innovation', *Research Policy*, vol. 6 (1977), 36–76; Wolfgang Zapf, 'On Social Innovations', Working Paper no. 254 (November 1987), Sonderforschungsbereich 3, Mikroanalytische Grundlagen der Gesellschaftspolitik, Frankfurt and Mannheim.

17 Pierre Bourdieu, *Distinction*, tr. R. Nice, London: Routledge & Kegan Paul, 1984.

18 Norbert Elias, *Über den Prozeß der Zivilisation*, vol. 2, Frankfurt: Suhrkamp, 1976; English translation *The Civilizing Process*, vol. 2 *State Formation and Civilization*, Oxford: Blackwell, 1982.

19 André Leroi-Gourhan, *Geste et la parole*; German translation see ch. 2, n. 29.

20 Michael Young, *The Metronomic Society: Natural Rhythms and Human Timetables*, London: Thames and Hudson, 1988.

21 Lewis Mumford, *Technics and Civilization*, New York: Harcourt, 1934, p. 42.

22 M. Melbin, *Night as Frontier*, New York: Free Press, 1987; J. E. McGrath and J. R. Kelly, *Time and Human Interaction: Toward a Social Psychology of Time*, New York: Guilford Press, 1986.

23 R. Herzog and R. Koselleck (eds), *Epochenschwelle und Epochenbewußtsein*, Munich: Wilhelm Fink Verlag, 1988.

24 Cacciari, *Zeit ohne Kronos*, p. 65.

25 Edmund Leach, 'Two Essays concerning the Symbolic Representation of Time', in: *Rethinking Anthropology*, London: Athlone Press, 1966.

Chapter 4 Politics of Time

1 Eviatar Zerubavel, *The Seven Day Circle: The History and Meaning of the Week*, New York: Free Press, 1985.

2 Massimo Cacciari, 'Erinnerung an Karneval', in: *Zeit ohne*

Kronos, Klagenfurt: Ritter Verlag, 1986, pp. 41–62.

3 Barbara Sichtermann, 'Wechselfälle', in: Rainer Zoll (ed.), *Zerstörung und Wiederaneignung von Zeit*, Frankfurt: Suhrkamp, 1988, pp. 641–55.

4 Fritz Scharpf, 'Strukturen der post-industriellen Gesellschaft', *Arbeit und Wirtschaft*, vol. 11, no. 1 (1985), 9–34.

5 Oskar Negt, *Lebendige Arbeit, enteignete Zeit: Politische und kulturelle Dimensionen des Kampfes um die Arbeitszeit*, Frankfurt: Campus, 1984.

6 Tom Schuller, 'Workending and Institutional Time: Employment, Impermanence and Ambiguity in the Life-Cycle', *Work and Society*, vol. 10 (1985).

7 Helga Nowotny, 'The Public and Private Uses of Time', in: Laura Balbo and Helga Nowotny (eds), *Time to Care in Tomorrow's Welfare Systems*, Vienna: Eurosocial, 1986.

8 Jürgen P. Rinderspacher, *Gesellschaft ohne Zeit: Individuelle Zeitverwendung und soziale Organisation der Arbeit*, Frankfurt: Campus, 1985; Giovanni Gasparini, *Il Tempo e il Lavoro*, Milan: Franco Angeli, 1986.

9 Helmut Wiesenthal, *Strategie und Illusion: Rationalitätsgrenzen kollektiver Akteure am Beispiel der Arbeitszeitpolitik 1980–1985*, Frankfurt: Campus, 1988.

10 Ibid.

11 Christiane Müller-Wichmann, *Zeitnot*, Weinheim: Beltz Verlag, 1984.

12 Eberhard K. Seifert, *Arbeitszeit in Deutschland: Herausbildung und Entwicklung industrieller Arbeitszeiten von der frühen Industrialisierung bis zum Kampf um die 35-Stunden-Woche*, dissertation, Fachbereich Wirtschaftswissenschaft, Wuppertal: Universität-Gesamthochschule Wuppertal, 1985; 'Zur Misere der amtlichen Arbeitszeitstatistik in Deutschland', *Archiv für Sozialgeschichte*, vol. XXVII (1987).

13 Wiesenthal, *Strategie und Illusion*.

14 Larry Hirschhorn, *Beyond Mechanization: Work and Technology in a Postindustrial Age*, Boston: MIT Press, 1984.

15 Helga Maria Hernes, *Welfare State and Woman Power: Essays in State Feminism*, Oslo: Norwegian University Press, 1987.

16 Seifert, *Arbeitszeit in Deutschland.*
17 Jesse Ausubel and A. Grübler, 'UK Working Time Indicators', Laxenburg: *IIASA* 1988, mimeo; P. J. Armstrong, 'Work, Rest or Play?', in: P. Marstrand (ed.), *New Technology and the Future of Work and Skills*, London: Frances Pinter, 1984.
18 Schuller, 'Workending and Institutional Time'.
19 Ausubel and Grübler, 'UK Working Time Indicators'.
20 Christian Lalive d'Epinay, 'Die soziale Ambivalenz der Freizeit', in: Rainer Zoll (ed.), *Zerstörung und Wiederaneignung von Zeit*, Frankfurt: Suhrkamp, 1988, p. 409.
21 Paul Lafargue, *Das Recht auf Faulheit und andere Satiren*, 1986. (Original 1887–8.)
22 Georges Bataille, *Die Aufhebung der Ökonomie*, Munich: Matthes & Seitz, 1985.
23 Müller-Wichmann, *Zeitnot.*
24 Hernes, *Welfare State and Woman Power.*
25 Peter M. M. Pritchard, 'Doctors, Patients and Time: A View from General Practice', in: R. Frankenberg (ed.), *Time and Health*, forthcoming.
26 A. Evers, H. Nowotny and H. Wintersberger (eds), *The Changing Face of Welfare*, Aldershot: Gower, 1987.
27 Laura Balbo, 'Crazy Quilts: Gesellschaftliche Reproduktion und Dienstleistungsarbeit', in: Ilona Kickbusch and Barbara Riedmüller (eds), *Die armen Frauen: Frauen und Sozialpolitik*, Frankfurt: Suhrkamp, 1984.
28 Wiesenthal, *Strategie und Illusion.*
29 Martin Lagergren et al., *Time to Care*, London: Pergamon, 1984.
30 Wiesenthal, *Strategie und Illusion.*
31 Ibid.

Chapter 5 The Longing for the Moment

1 Niklas Luhmann, 'Die Knappheit der Zeit und die Vordringlichkeit des Befristeten', *Verwaltung*, vol. I (1968), p. 13; 'Weltzeit und Systemgeschichte', in: *Soziologische*

Aufklärung, vol. 2, Opladen: Westdeutscher Verlag, 1973; *Vertrauen: Ein Mechanismus zur Reduktion sozialer Komplexität*, 2nd edn, Stuttgart: F. Enke, 1973; 'Temporalisierung und Komplexität: Zur Semantik neuzeitlicher Zeitbegriffe', in: *Gesellschaftsstruktur und Semantik*, vol. I, Frankfurt: Suhrkamp, 1980.

2 T. C. Schelling, 'Foreword', in: *Time in Economic Life*, *Quarterly Journal of Economics*, vol. 4 (1973), p. 627; Staffan Burenstam Linder, *The Hurried Leisure Class*, New York: Columbia University Press, 1970; Jacob Mincer, 'Market Prices, Opportunity Costs, and Income Effects', in: Carl F. Christ et al. (eds), *Measurement in Economics*, Stanford: Stanford University Press, 1963.

3 Luhmann, 'Die Knappheit der Zeit'.

4 Michael Young, *The Metronomic Society: Natural Rhythms and Human Timetables*, London: Thames and Hudson, 1988, p. 217.

5 Christiane Müller-Wichmann, *Zeitnot*, Weinheim: Beltz Verlag, 1984.

6 Young, *Metronomic Society*.

7 Reinhart Koselleck, *op. cit.*

8 See, for example, Willy Bierter et al., *Keine Zukunft für lebendige Arbeit?*, Stuttgart: C. E. Poeschl, 1988; Oskar Negt, *Lebendige Arbeit, enteignete Zeit*, Frankfurt: Campus, 1984.

9 Dietmar Kamper and Christoph Wulf (eds), *Die sterbende Zeit*, Darmstadt: Luchterhand, 1987.

10 Young, *Metronomic Society*.

11 Klaus Laermann, 'Alltags-Zeit', in: Rainer Zoll (ed.), *Zerstörung und Wiederaneignung von Zeit*, Frankfurt: Suhrkamp, 1988, p. 339.

12 Barbara Sichtermann, 'Wechselfälle', in: Zoll, *Zerstörung*, pp. 644–5.

13 Ibid., p. 655.

14 See the interesting self-portrait of an addict here. Henri Bents, 'Computerarbeit und Lebenszeit', in: Zoll, *Zerstörung*, pp. 293–303.

15 Jürgen P. Rinderspacher, *Gesellschaft ohne Zeit*, Frankfurt: Campus, 1985; Willy Hohn, *Die Zerstörung der Zeit*, Frankfurt: Fischer Verlag, 1984.

16 Rom Harré (ed.), *The Social Construction of Emotions*, Oxford: Blackwell, 1986.

17 Helmut Wiesenthal, *Strategie und Illusion: Rationalitätsgrenzen kollektiver Akteure am Beispiel der Arbeitszeitpolitik 1980–1985*, Frankfurt: Campus, 1988.

18 Richard Larson, 'Perspectives on Queues: Social Justice and the Psychology of Queueing', *Operations Research*, 1988.

19 A. Astruc and M. Contat, *Sartre: Ein Film*, Paris, 1977, quoted from Blumenberg, p. 311.

20 Miyamoto Musaki, *Book of Five Rings*, London: Allison & Busby, 1974.

21 Laermann, 'Alltags-Zeit', p. 340; Jean Piaget, *Die Bildung des Zeitbegriffs beim Kinde*, Stuttgart: Klett-Cotta, 1980.

22 Caroline Neubaur, *Übergänge: Spiel und Realität in der Psychoanalyse Donald W. Winnicotts*, Frankfurt: Athenäum, 1987, pp. 83–4.

23 Pierre Bourdieu, 'La société traditionelle, attitude à l'égard du temps et conduite économique', *Sociologie du Travail*, vol. I (1963), 24–44.

24 Norbert Elias, *Über die Zeit*, Frankfurt: Suhrkamp, 1984, pp. 112–13.

25 Mark Elchardus, 'The Rediscovery of Chronos: The New Role of Time in Sociological Theory', *International Sociology*, vol. 3, no. I (March 1988), 35–60.

26 Reinhart Koselleck, 'Erfahrungswandel und Methodenwechsel: Eine historische-anthropologische Skizze', in: *Theorie der Geschichte*, 1988, pp. 51–2.

27 Jack Goody, *The Domestication of the Savage Mind*, Cambridge: Cambridge University Press, 1977.

28 Oskar Ozlak, on the period of military dictatorship in Argentina. Verbal communication.

29 Elias, *Über die Zeit*, pp. 91–2.

30 Henri Atlan, *A Tort et à Raison: Intercritique de la science et du mythe*, Paris: Editions du Seuil, 1986, p. 268.

31 Massimo Cacciari, *Zeit ohne Kronos*, Klagenfurt: Ritter Verlag, 1986, pp. 138–9.

32 Neubaur, *Übergänge*, pp. 93, 108.

33 Ilya Prigogine and Isabelle Stengers, *Entre le Temps et l'Eternité*, Paris: Fayard, 1988.
34 Stephen W. Hawking, *A Brief History of Time: From the Big Bang to Black Holes*, London: Bantham Press, 1988.

Index

Index by Jennifer Speake